MW00897831

Yeshua's Yoga:

The Non-Dual Consciousness Teachings of the Gospel of Thomas

by

Kimberly Beyer-Nelson, MA

Cover design by Kathy Haug
http://ferncreekassociates.com/

Other Titles by Kimberly Beyer-Nelson:

A Little Book of Wholeness and Prayer: An Eight-Week Journaling Companion
(Skinner House Books)

Easing into The Bhagavad-Gita and Patanjali's Yoga Sutras
(also in Kindle and Audio editions)

At Matthew's Knee: A Poetic Commentary on the Gospel of Matthew
(also in Kindle and Audio editions)

Acknowledgements

Where does an idea first
send down roots,
tentative, blind,
and then push up, unfurling?
What forms of sun and mist and water droplets
nurture such a thing?
Am I the maker of my own ideas,
or do they stretch, all of them,
back along a genealogical line
with more knots than
straight threads?

Maybe we only see the pattern
later,
at a distance.
Or maybe such things
were never meant to be teased out—
we are only to trust the support
of fibers
like the weave of
a sweet summer hammock.

Thank you—
Sue Sutherland-Hanson for companioning and proofing
Tom Thresher for allowing
Lynn Bauman for teaching
my parents for encouraging
Francis Gross for sowing ideas long ago
Sound Spirit learning groups in Suquamish for questioning
Sophia Circle of Poulsbo for framing it with silence
Kathy Haug for thinking in color
and all the ones who
smiled politely
when I raved
about
things like beauty, truth and the interconnection of all things.
This seed found form and was nurtured by you all.

Important Reminders As We Begin Our Journey Together

The poet must submit to the strain of holding in balance present circumstances and glimpsed alternatives.
--Seamus Heaney

Only the hand that erases can write the true thing.
--Meister Eckhart

For everything you have missed you have gained something else.
--Ralph Waldo Emerson

You are going through all this emotional upheaval because your coziness has been, in some small or large way, addressed.
--Pema Chodron

Searching for him took
my strength.
One night I bent
my pointing finger—
Never such a moon.
--Keppo

It is a joy to be hidden but a disaster not to be found.
--D.W. Winnicott

You cease to impose and you discover.
--Charles Tomlinson

The function of the imagination is not to make strange things settled but to make settled things strange.
--G.K. Chesterton

Forward

Rev. Dr. Thomas Thresher
author of
Reverent Irreverence

We in the West, steeped as we are in the Occidental perception of the world, find the Gospel of Thomas to be a mysterious, compelling text. It has no story line, just sayings that challenge our yearning for closure. It is simultaneously mysterious and familiar. It touches briefly on the biblical gospels and then darts away. If we are fans of Eastern perspectives, we recognize a kindred soul in Thomas. Yet he remains foreign. We wonder--how can we understand the Gospel of Thomas? But the question misses the point. The question is, how will *we* be changed?

I am a reluctant Christian, one who came to the faith through strange encounters. None of those encounters included the Jesus of Western Christianity. When I came upon Thomas' Gospel, I discovered a home I hadn't imagined. Suddenly, I had a powerful lens on the Western tradition I had been called to serve. Just as suddenly, my passion for Eastern spirituality had a bridge to the West. Thomas held just enough ambiguity, just enough of East and West, to allow me to stand in both worlds and find a home.

When, during a four-day retreat, Lynn Bauman suggested that the second logion of Thomas was a map of the spiritual journey and, in fact, might reveal Yeshua's own journey, I was entranced. For years I had taught that the Christian liturgical year was just such a spiritual map. But here was Yeshua's Way spelled out in Logion 2: seek and you will find; when you find you will be troubled; stay in trouble and you will open to wonder; in awe and wonder you will find mastery; and your mastery will be your rest. Wow! Here was a Christian explanation of awakening, standing in stark contrast to a tradition that seemed to shut down exploration in favor of too-small answers. It was liberating! I began and continue to teach Thomas to my church.

I argued in my book, *Reverent Irreverence*, that churches are uniquely positioned to lead the evolution of human consciousness in these times of great need. Using the lens of Integral Theory, I stressed two pivotal avenues for this task: enlarging our culture's orienting ontological story and deepening our personal reflection. The Gospel of Thomas furthers both.

Despite the decline of Christianity in the West, it still "owns" the great Myth that orients our individual purpose. If we are to inspire more expansive ways of knowing and caring, we must use the church's authority to expand this great Myth. If we are to reflect upon our own evolution, we need a fresh lens through which to see ourselves. The Gospel of Thomas is a vehicle for both; it pushes at the edge of our culture's story of who we are and why we are here, then challenges our deepest assumptions. Thomas is just foreign enough to invite us to question our traditional understanding of Christianity but familiar enough to not lose us.

What has been missing is a systematic presentation bringing together the most provocative understanding of Thomas while inviting deep, personal exploration. Kim is a consummate teacher, so who better to advance the Gospel of Thomas as the stunning teaching tool it is? Using poetry, reason, sacred insight, and spiritual practice, Kim provides a pragmatic and engaging pathway into this Gospel. Every passage is infused with her passion for direct knowing. As a teacher, she invites us to experience each logion from multiple orientations, not so that you will understand it, but so it *might change you*. Dive in and enjoy!

Tom Thresher

Forward

Sue Sutherland-Hanson, M. Div.
author (with Kimberly Beyer-Nelson, MA) of
An Invitation to Openness: Poems for Individuals and Communities Living in the Present Moment

Reading the Gospel of Thomas can open the door to our own deep wisdom as well as the Transcendent beyond, but like all sacred texts, many of the logia in this little treasure can leave us scratching our heads. Here is where a poetic *and* researched response like Kimberly's provides a valuable study aid. But to leave you with the idea that *Yeshua's Yoga* is primarily a scholarly work would be inaccurate. All sacred texts merit study, but adding the gaze of the heart and spirit is the surest way to bathe in their transformational wisdom. This book helps you soak in the Gospel of Thomas.

There are good reasons why poets are often grouped with prophets. They both incline their ears to hear *and* they speak with the heart-language of God. I picture Kim holding a candle and chatting while we readers feel our way along the logia as we might in winding tunnels under dark, ancient, and sacred grounds.

I spent much of my time reading Kim's book in the warmth of the summer sun at the backyard picnic table. There I often found myself sighing in joy at Yeshua's vision of reality.

This brings me to my summation of the Gospel of Thomas: a) the news *is* good   b) our work is to see and act on that "good" reality as Yeshua did.

Kimberly's collection is timely support for the 1945 discovery of the Gospel of Thomas. I think of a recent conversation with my yoga teacher and friend, Suzanne. Suzanne grew up Catholic and was searching for ways to revitalize her faith. She discovered a Hindu author, Paramahansa Yogananda, who helped her see the electrifying immediacy of Christ's teaching through the light of Eastern Wisdom. She lent me one of his books in which I read, "The Great Christ, radiating the spiritual strength and power of the Orient to the West, is a divine liaison to unite God-loving peoples of East and West."[1]   It lifts my spirits to hear Yeshua revered by yet another wise man of the East, but I was not as surprised as Suzanne thought I would be. I had already met the wisdom that Yogananda described in the Gospel of Thomas.

The gnosis of the Gospel of Thomas levels its focus to the deep unitive centers of yogis, poets, and seekers from all over the world longing to find meaning, a path, and for many American Christians, relevancy. Yogananda accurately speaks of the Gospel of Thomas beaming with the Eastern wisdom of Yeshua. My friend, Suzanne's spiritual journey reflects the experience of many modern day seekers and reinforces my suspicion that the timing of the uncovering of the Gospel of Thomas is... well, a God-thing.

There are several key reasons that the timing of the rediscovery of The Gospel of Thomas appears to be divinely intentional. One, our modern world with its technology has brought the West and East closer than ever. Cross-pollination of the great Faith traditions has increased our ability to interpret the sayings of Yeshua, who was an Eastern teacher himself.

On a darker note, technology has ushered us into an era where we have the capability to destroy creation and each other. Perhaps our most important defense arises from humans recognizing their unity in God with both wisdom and compassion. In this, the power of Christ's transformational and shocking teachings as they appear in the Gospel of Thomas are particularly timely.

Lucky you. You are about to join an intimate and inspiring tryst with Kim and the Spirit of the Christ. You are sure to enjoy the company. And yet, don't be surprised if you find yourself reveling in the divine embrace of the One. This is what one should expect from the Gospel of Thomas seen through the eyes of a poet, a prophet, a friend, and the Divine wisdom of your own heart.

Sue Sutherland-Hanson

Works Cited

1-*The Yoga of Jesus,* Paramahansa Yogananda p. 15

An Introductory Essay to the Hermeneutics of the Gospel of Thomas by Lynn Bauman,

author of

The Gospel of Thomas: Wisdom of the Twin

The small Gospel text, called the *Gospel of Thomas*, was discovered with a trove of other ancient documents in a buried library at Nag Hammadi, Egypt in the middle of the last century. Its discovery has had a profound effect on modern biblical scholarship and is making a deep impact on the thinking of contemporary Christians.

The Gospel of Thomas was found in the precise form that many scholars had imagined the first Christian documents to be—a list of the sayings of Jesus, called ***logoi sophon***, or "wise sayings" from a spiritual master. It was believed that the first students and chroniclers of Jesus would have collected his words and stories into short lists as they began to disappear from history.

Until the Gospel of Thomas was discovered, we did not have a sayings collection. The thought in contemporary scholarship is that the Gospel of Thomas represents a list important to Aramaic and Syriac speakers who lived to the East of Palestine. These Christians had, of course, been influenced by

Thomas as his work and teachings spread all the way to India and China.

These 114 sayings are made up of aphorisms and parables unique in many ways. First, they appear to be primitive or unembellished in form, and second, about half of them are new to the western canonical tradition of Christianity. At first glance, it appeared that the arrangement of these sayings was entirely random. But now, after further consideration, it seems that not only is there a deliberate arrangement to the collection, but there is also an underlying theme that holds it together devoted to the idea of oneness (or unity) which John's Gospel also captures in John 17:22—*I have given them the glory that you gave me, that they may be one as we are one.* Furthermore, from a contemporary point of view in modern hermeneutical theory, there seems to be an internal semiotic structure that binds the text together in more hidden ways, and which constellates the various sayings around six important themes.

The clue to this internal structure is found in the second logion which lists the six salient states of wisdom which Jesus outlines in his teaching and through which the seeker must pass through in order to experience the full impact of wisdom. Using them perhaps as a heuristic, these six states can provide centers around which this document can be read and better understood. While not exactly explicit, they are implied throughout the text and provide a valuable lens through which to explore the Gospel and the wisdom teachings they embody.

Let me outline what I understand the six states of wisdom from Logion 2 to be. They are critical to this study and the approach taken by the volume you hold in your hands. The first two states, **searching** and **finding**, are common to the ancient Jewish tradition and found both in the canonical Gospels and in the Hebrew Scriptures. Wisdom seekers are urged to actively participate in the discovery of wisdom. In this injunction to search, there should be no let up until one has the experience of finding that for which one seeks. In fact, the traditional assurance to the seeker is that one will indeed find if one pursues a serious search.

The next two states, **trouble** and **wonder,** appear to be new to the tradition and were introduced to the search for wisdom as a result of Jesus' own spiritual journey. Finding, in Jesus' view, is not the end of the story. In fact, finding is in some ways provisional—what one finds may open up entirely new doors and questions that leave one in a state of confusion (or trouble). Finding is not always conclusive. The first finding may be simply the first step in a much longer process, and so it will leave us baffled and in wonderment at least initially. However, the text suggests that if we will stay with our confusion, and not try to hide or deny it, we will be rewarded with breakthroughs that will result in a new state of awe or wonder. We begin to see, perhaps, the wider picture. We are privileged to discover more than just the initial finding.

These initial states require a further step: **reigning** or mastery. In any new field we attempt to learn, we do not truly know the territory until we somehow master its complexities. To "reign like a king or queen" in any endeavor is to practice it long enough so it becomes a part of our own being—a part of our life. This is a form of sovereignty that one observes in any competent master of a special art, a sport well played, or any complex skill. Not until we master it do we "reign" over it, or (perhaps better) through it.

From such sovereignty, then, the sixth and final state arises—**rest**. One can be at peace or in a state of rest in the midst of complex activity. A "master" can use the skill or field of knowledge with ease. It looks effortless because that individual has mastered the skill and is inwardly at rest. Something of this process seems to be at the heart of this whole Gospel.

The hundred and fourteen logia appear to be about these six states and the questions and concerns they each raise. When one has completed the cycle, however, it appears that the cycle begins all over again, instigating new searches and findings.

In this volume, Kimberly Beyer-Nelson has centered her explorations around what I believe to be the central concern of its Gospel—the wisdom of oneness (or non-duality). Then she has done (and is ably demonstrating) what every student of this unique stream of wisdom *must* do—making the text and its principles her own by wrestling with its truth and integrating its meaning as an integral and practical part of her own life. Her work is a template for others who would *seek to grasp* (as Thomas says in the opening Logion) *the meaning of this text in order to transcend the taste of death*. I am pleased that she is pioneering this genre of wisdom-seeking and finding as a personal process and has produced a volume to encourage others in the same heart-felt work.

Lynn Bauman
July 2014

Introduction

Welcome to the Gospel of Thomas

In December of 1945, a remarkable discovery in the desert near Nag-Hammadi came to light, held for centuries within the huge cliffs that ripple out along the Nile River in Upper Egypt. Safely cradled in a huge earthen jar rested thirteen papyrus books and within one of those books, the complete Gospel of Thomas.

Fragments had been found at other archeological sites over the years, usually in Greek. The unearthing of the entire manuscript, however, was a watershed event. Unlike the Gospels of the Bible, Thomas was composed as a simple list of sayings, bare of almost any narrative. Written in Coptic, scholars are unsure if the original had once been penned in Greek, Syriac, and Aramaic. Many of the sayings are quite similar to the words of Jesus preserved in the Synoptic Gospels (Matthew, Mark, Luke and John) but often with interesting "twists" of language that illustrate a different intent. Because of this, scholars tend to link the Gospel of Thomas with other documents like the still un-earthed "Q" or *Quella* (Source), which has been posited as a kind of feeder document for the content of the Synoptic Gospels. Generally, the Gospel of Thomas is thought to pre-date the Gospels of the Bible because of its lack of narrative form and it seems quite independent of the Christological trajectory of Matthew, Mark, Luke and John.

In short, it is a fascinating and frustrating piece of literature, just enough like our Biblical ideas of who Yeshua (Jesus) was and yet wholly different at the same time. In its pages, you will not find miracles, revealed prophesies, healings or the passion story. Instead, you will meet a breathing Wisdom teacher, whose words often serve as koans and who walked fully as a man engaged both with this world and the Divine simultaneously, an *ihidaya* or "unified one".

What translation and why

I have chosen to use through-out this work the powerful words penned by Lynn Bauman called *The Gospel of Thomas: Wisdom of the Twin* (second ed). This translation, as well as its commentaries, captures the energy and intent of the Gospel in a language that is both poetic and accessible. His work with the meta-frame that over-arches the seemingly random sayings of Yeshua, reflected in the care and scholarship so evident in his essay at the beginning of this particular book, has been instrumental to my better understanding of this ancient text.

The Invitation To You, the Reader

This, however, is not a book of scholarly intent alone, but rather a work that explores the non-dual or unitive consciousness teachings that are the very soul of this document and one of the reasons why scholars have struggled with its seemingly random and, to many of them, nonsensical sayings. Unless you are able to meet Yeshua as a kind of Middle Eastern Zen Master or Jnana (Wisdom) Yogi, you will miss most of what he is trying to say. All the logia are couched in metaphoric language and all are bent on one incredible idea: through deep and heart-felt relationship with the entire cosmos, we come into our own as beings continuous with the God we often try to hold outside and above ourselves. We are called again and again to see the world in a kind of bifocal arrangement, never separating ourselves from the flow of life and its "ten-thousand things", a view called "relative reality" and at the same time, never missing the ground of all being, "ultimate reality", that is just as much a part of our existence. The work makes sacred *everything* of the creation, even as it indicts the institutions, political and religious, that keep people from standing up and claiming that knowledge and blessing. If it was taken deeply to heart as the original Christian canon came together, The Gospel of Thomas would *not* have stood as tool that would have made building institutional churches and empires easy. The seat of heaven, for

Yeshua, is consciousness--our way of seeing or not seeing that the Kingdom is already spread out around us and within us. We alone are responsible for standing up and living out of that kind of knowledge or gnosis. This is not a view of life that leads to hierarchical power structures.

Why is this point so important? Let's pause here and think about four powerful ideas: material/institutional religion, the symbolic elements of belief, the relational elements of belief, and faith as such and put them in the non-dual or unitive framework.

The Four Breast-Plates of Union

Several years ago, I stumbled across a lovely way of looking at differences between faith and belief, as well as the mental polarities that exist between spirit and religion and dual and non-dual consciousness. It is called *The Four Breastplates* and has its origins in the Sufi tradition of Islam. It goes something like this:

1. Your first breastplate consists of all the *material pieces of your religion*: altars, crosses, vestments, professional religious certifications, buildings, musical instruments, pews, etc. These things may change over time and can

be taken from you because they are part of the nature of our impermanent and ultimately fragile world.

2. Your second breastplate consists of all the *symbolic elements of belief*: the well-turned sermon, scripture, dogmas, creeds, hymns, prayers, mental and verbal beliefs, prayers and images we hold. All these may morph over time and can cease to have meaning for you because they, too, are grounded in a reality that changes.

3. Your third breastplate is *wholly relational*, and is typified by experience and interactions and questions. We begin to ask what is *my* relationship with God? We start to feel rather than simply think, discern rather than blindly accept, experience and walk with rather than follow. We enter into conversation, into companionship, into discipleship with both others and our God. We respond to the divine as father, teacher, companion, and lover. But once again, these relational elements can change over time and become unsatisfactory because they are grounded in charged language, images, thoughts, imagination, and memories. In other words, relationship is based in relative reality that sees beginnings and endings, good and bad, walking with and walking apart. Relationship is not the Truth in its ultimate sense, merely

a critical icon that allows us to catch those first and fleeting glimpses of Union.

4. Your fourth breastplate is *unity with* God, the living ground of our being: *"and it is no longer I who live, but Christ lives in me..."* (Galatians 2:20b). This is the breastplate that cannot be taken from you because it is *who you are at your core.* This is the breastplate that Thomas Merton called the True Self, and others have named enlightenment, awakening, Self-Realization and many other words and phrases we have tried to pin to it. It's pure experience, pure being, and we have to slip back up to the second and third breastplates when we want to share it with others or even talk about it to ourselves. And when we try to do that, we will all, at some level, utterly fail.

Christianity has not been good at teaching the third and fourth breastplates, except through the hints given to us by our mystics and contemplatives. This is the state of mind The Gospel of Thomas' Yeshua lived in and calls us to find. It's understandable that we don't hear of this on Sunday mornings because it cannot really be given or taught *directly*. Language fails in the fourth breastplate, utterly and delightfully. The experience is simply NOW, and afterwards, it puts all our belief in fact-based knowing, time, and space into a tizzy.

Our culture is in a period of tremendous and exciting change as it begins to find ways to ask us to live out of *each* of the breastplates, relying on them on different occasions even as we begin to manifest that fourth experiential breastplate. It's fascinating that the Gospel of Thomas may be one of the best documents we have about Jesus' teachings about his own inner spiritual journey, a path that is grounded in the state of non-dual consciousness. How incredible that it was found at a time in history when it could actually be understood and used by those of us in the West. With the influx of teachers and writings from Buddhism, Sikhism, Vedanta and the various Yogas of India and the work of philosophical Taoism to name just a few sources, as well as great translations of the pre-Nicean Church Fathers, Syrian church writers, and mystics, we are prepared in a way almost no Western culture and time has been to hear the depth of this important scripture. Add to that treasury our own contemporary writers and teachers like nationally known Thomas Merton, Richard Rohr, Adayashanti and simple local pastors like Tom Thresher and others who are actively engaged with the work of bringing non-dual consciousness to light in us and our culture and we can begin to see that the opportunity for this Gospel to be read as one of the brightest illuminations of the Way of Jesus has finally dawned.

The Structure of *Yeshua's Yoga*

As I sat down to work with the Gospel of Thomas each day, I followed a time-tested contemplative technique called *Lectio Divina* (Divine Reading). First, I spoke the logion of the day out loud, just getting a sense of its literal meaning, tone and cadence. Then I sat in silence, holding that experience.

When it felt right, I read it a second time, with an ear to what it was saying to *me* --the me who studies Eastern Philosophy, the me who loves liturgical church services, the me who is a long-time Centering Prayer practitioner, the me who is mother, artist, writer, animal lover, Yoga instructor, messy housekeeper, on and on. In other words, I brought all of myself to the table and listened to what pieces of myself perked up and paid attention. These messages to the bits and pieces of myself were seldom literal. They often couched themselves in the language of metaphor. Again, I waited in silence for a while.

Finally, I read it one more time, allowing myself to settle down with a single luminous word or phrase. Until I felt quiet inside, I didn't feel ready to respond further. Sometimes that is all I accomplished that particular day—no writing, no making sense of anything. I let the words tag around with me as I went on to other things—laundry, teaching, playing with some of the other writing I was doing. I let the words cook in me until I could digest them more fully.

When the urge hit, a few minutes or few days later, I responded to the logion with a poem. This, for me, is the first language of transcribing experiential events in a form that I can share with others. Poetry occupies the same energetic space as music, art, and dance—it communicates effectively, even as it leaves vast amounts of space around the notes, the words, the images, and the movements, inviting others into an intimate relationship that is the core of meaning-making. It gives me room to be both playful and metaphorical, matching the logion in a dialogue that is in tune with what I had heard and walked around with, but bringing it alive for my particular time and place. It is, I suppose, like participating in a kind of resurrection.

Next, I tried to speak to folks who like things a little more concrete and rational. Sometimes that shift was hard—from logion to poetry to prose, and sometimes it felt absolutely natural. The work of exegesis is the ongoing dance with the words that come to us from other places and times, often in languages other than our own. Without careful and prayerful discernment, without struggling with the words in common prose, we begin to lose the efficacy of the original words and their ability to impact our place and time, to be the very energy of a transformative and lived Way. Because we often work with translations of translations, particularly in the Christian tradition, this work is doubly important. Literalism is so very foreign to the way Jesus taught, and so by going deeper, by applying and critically examining the layers of meaning and intention in scripture, we more fully align ourselves with the "come, let us reason" (Isaiah 1:18) *and our own heart-felt intuitions and feelings,* which is how we are called to respond to all of life by this Wisdom teacher named Yeshua.

That movement of exegesis often took me into the other avenues of my own training as a comparative religionist. I added voices from both the Buddhist and Yogic traditions because, for me, there is so much resonance and a sophisticated depth of understanding there--another language, if you will, for what Yeshua was conveying in parable and metaphor and analogies appropriate for his own time and place. Unlike some Christians who are threatened by Jesus sharing the page with the great teachers, poets, saints and avatars of India and Tibet, Turkey, Japan, China and Vietnam, I find the similar melodies deeply comforting. The words seem to stand as witness that what Yeshua had discovered was nothing other than what great spiritual masters in many times and places had discovered—that God and human and indeed all of creation, is One, and we are called to be an *ihidaya*, a "unified one", like Jesus himself. Like a kind of scientific validation that comes when an experiment is repeatable, I was profoundly moved to find the nearly word for word echoes of the experiences of Yeshua in the awakened lives of other human beings. These traditions also know and appreciate in their various ways the idea of *Ishvarapranidhana*, the concept that each of us will chose for ourselves that one form and idea of God that will be our icon, our window, into Ultimate Reality. Jesus is that teacher, that form, that Icon for me.

But it is never enough to keep spiritual ideas like a set of playing cards, dragging them out when the mood suits, entertaining and consoling as the need arises. That is the very epitome of a dualistic mindset. So I tried, each day, to ask questions that challenged me to manifest in little ways the wisdom I was learning. It was a technique to test the reality of the words I was hearing, put the teachings into practice, and to evaluate if this was indeed a valid and life-give Way. That, to me, is the proof of the spiritual pudding, so to speak: can the path be *walked* rather than simply thought about? Can it be made concrete and relational instead of abstract and singular and lifeless?

In the end, you will have to be the judge of that for yourself.

Finally, I tried to sum up, in one simple line, the intent of the logion. I did this primarily to see if, at the end of each section of searching, finding, trouble, wonder, reigning and rest, I would have a sort of sutra of the Gospel of Thomas—a set of one-line jewels that point back to the work itself in a way that is easily digested and held in total. I liked the resulting collection of one-liners from each logion because I found it easier to see the incredible layering of teachings in this gospel holistically. It is not a document of random sayings at all, but rather, a document that lays out the path of Jesus in a way that I believe *is* rational, livable and incredibly wise.

So, I'm sharing this journey with you now. I'm not going to claim it is the only way to read this ancient document, but I think you will find enough exciting, stimulating and thoughtful ideas that you may be encouraged to take a similar trip with Yeshua for a time. I hope that it changes your life as much as it has changed (and continues to change) my own.

Ameyn! (An Aramaic form of Amen, meaning "this is the ground of my connection with Unity, from which all my actions will flow").

A final thought for us all:

I who know and do not know that I know:
Let me be whole.
Let me be awake.

I who have known, but do not know:
Let me once more see
the beginning of it all.

I who do not wish to know,
but still say that I wish to know:
Let me be guided
to safety and light.

I who do not know and
know that I do not know:
let me through this knowledge, know.

I who do knot know, but think I know:
set me free
from the confusion
of that ignorance.

(Anonymous Islamic Prayer)

The First Movement:
The Logia about Searching

Logion 1

I who write this am Thomas
the Double, the Twin.
Yeshua, the Living Master spoke,
and his secret sayings I have
written down.

I assure you, whoever grasps their
meaning will not know the taste
of death.

First Response:

My mind wandered
until I realized how I taste death,
from this carrot to that fish,
from this apple to that fat hen,
how I swirl with it,
taking in what was once out,
giving life to what had become
lifeless,
facing
with my own mortality
an indisputable truth:
there is no top of the food chain—
only and eternally
relationship.

Today in Wisdom's Caravan:

Sometimes the Gospel of Thomas is often viewed as a
very individualistic approach to faith, a kind of Middle Eastern
Jnana (Wisdom) Yoga. This idea of the solitary, insular path is

often cited as one of the reasons why the Gospel did not make the cut at the Council of Nicea where the Christian Canon was set. But throughout the work, there are intimations of community, of a reality that can only be told through the many voices that unite to form unity. Even here at the beginning, relationship seems to be key. The idea of the twin, the intertwining of lives both material and spiritual co-created in the womb of life sets the tone for the entire work.

Sufi and language scholar, Neil Douglas-Klotz, writes that we might think of time as a caravan. The oldest moments of our shared history are before us on the trail and thus we look forward to our beginnings. We stand in the holy present moment on that path, the middle of the caravan, and behind us comes the future, still defining and unveiling itself in response to our moment-to-moment actions. What has happened and what will happen are simply part of that Now, so the words of Yeshua are fresh, alive, and vitally informing the living center of the entire caravan—us. And thus we pass the energy of creation back down the line.

To speak, to enunciate and thus bring into manifestation, is part of the function of holy wisdom, which might be seen as the energetic and creative aspect of divine reality. To speak these logia aloud brings us into twin-ship with Yeshua as we share his breath, the very vibration if you will, of his wisdom teachings.

Ameyn.

The Eastern Parallels:

"Two birds, beautiful of wing, close companions, cling to one common tree. Of the two, one eats the sweet fruit of that tree, the other eats not but watches his companion. The self is the bird that sits immersed on the common tree, but because he is not Lord, he is bewildered and has sorrow. But when he sees that other who is the Lord and the beloved, he knows that all is His greatness and his sorrow passes away from him. When, a seer, he sees the Golden-hued One, the Maker, the Lord, the Spirit who is the source of Brahman, then he becomes the knower and shakes from his wings sin and virtue. Pure of all stains, he reaches supreme identity."

--Mundaka Upanisha, Aurobindo Trans.

Going Deeper:

Breathe in the sense of a womb, saying "yes" to holy wisdom. Breathe out a sense of birthing a raying out of that space with possibility and light.

Summation:

To Search means to prepare to enter into relationship.

Logion 2

Yeshua says,

"If you are searching
you must not stop
until you find.
When you find, however,
you will be troubled.
Your confusion will give way to wonder.
In wonder you will reign over all things.
Your sovereignty will be your rest."

First Response:

I admit it.
I want to go to the last line first—
impatience is the tone of my age after all,
and rest?
delicious and guilty-dubious at once.
Maybe a pregnant restlessness is part of silence.
Searching and finding never seem to fill;
trouble and reigning sound tiring;
so yes, I'm already wondering,
wandering.
Can I learn to walk a path in a way that does not
anticipate an end
before
it
begins?

Today in Wisdom's Caravan:

I have always been intrigued with the energy informing
our first impulse to search at all. In the Gospel of Thomas, that
energy might be seen as the ripples we continue to ride after

that first act of creation, a way the Word and the only I AM vibrate within us, calling us forward and inward.

In a sense, this second logion shows how we are called to explore, to create, to understand. It's built into us with that word MUST. We will be drawn through the stages of searching, finding, trouble, wonder, reigning and rest, as well as the deep silence when the phrases and concepts all fall away.

Yeshua plays with words here though. His understanding of searching, finding, being troubled, experiencing wonder, reigning and rest will purposefully tip the ground beneath our feet. Even when he uses the word "stand", something he does throughout this Gospel, the Coptic actually means something like "stand as a preparation to move". In this, perhaps, the modern reader can feel the same energy the Buddha exuded, and whose itinerant lifestyle echoed the very same message—there is never a real stopping place on this journey. The caravan moves on eternally.

If I am sensitive to the melody of relationship, I will find it here in this logion both implicitly and explicitly. Part of our search is typically relating to the words, rituals and the personal spiritual practices of others. Finding leads us into trouble because it very often throws our relationship with all those sources of tangible "right ways" into doubt. We see here our dance with people and institutions requires us to practice discernment, to trust our intuitive and creative selves that may not agree with those powers and communities or even the beliefs or practices of our very closest friends. But then, we finally emerge from our time of trouble and enter into a kind of wonder where, very often, we find new levels of energy in the very words, rituals and forms that we thought we might have to abandon. We begin to relate to the institutions and the people in our lives in new ways. We begin to reign, to sit with a royal ease in this new paradigm we have discovered, but we are never alone in this. Notice Yeshua isn't laying out a lonely hermit's path here—reigning will call us to engage and interact even as we recognize the inherent nobility of each person we meet. Even that royal ease that leads to rest will be fully entwined with all of life and with others. That is the secret of its dynamic wholeness.

Ameyn.

The Eastern Parallels:

"When I first entered the stream
mountains were mountains and rivers were rivers.
Then one day,
mountains were no longer mountains and
rivers were no longer rivers.
Finally, after many years of practice,
mountains are again mountains
and rivers are again rivers."

--Zen Master Dogen

Going Deeper:

Breathe in a felt sense of curiosity. Breathe out a felt sense of sharing this curiosity with all of life.

Summation:

To Search means to be actively open to a transformation of consciousness and a new way of relating with others.

Logion 3

Yeshua says,

"If your spiritual guides say to you,
'Look, the divine Realm is
in the sky,'
well, then, the birds
will get there ahead of you.
If they say,
'It is in the sea,'
then the fish will precede you.

No, divine Reality exists
inside and around you.

Only when you have come to know
your true Self will you be fully known—
realizing at last that you
are a child of the Living One.
If, however, you never come to know who you
truly are,
you are a poverty-stricken being
and it is your 'self'
which lies impoverished."

First Response:

Wisdom has no single place in sky or sea,
no one place to rest its head on the earth
because
all places vibrate with it,
a spinning yin-yang
we can only glimpse
when we jerk it down

41

into blacks and whites.
But I challenge you:
lean toward the gray,
toward the dust of the caravan ahead of you,
and feel the wind of process and paradox.
We are not called to merely sit,
staring,
but to dance.

Today in Wisdom's Caravan:

"*If your spiritual guides say to you*" is an immediate wake-up call to us. This phrase points to the incompleteness of knowledge that is only heard, not experienced or lived from within us. The danger of such things is that we might look to where such teachers point, thinking that is the whole answer. Or worse, we may believe that by watching their proverbial finger, we can somehow participate in their experience. In truth, such knowledge will never equal our own breathing and dynamic approach to mystery.

The inner teacher, the still small voice within us, is also the note that rings through all creation. So to see the state of our personal sovereignty located somewhere above or below us, outside of us in other words, is not wrong per se, simply incomplete. It needs to ripen further. As our own senses begin to resonate with the presence of the divine both around us as well as within us, we come to a much clearer understanding of who we really are.

And that self/Self understanding is a movement that is filled with everything, with all possibilities, with that first creative energy that still illuminates all matter. It is the opposite of poverty because it is every fullness. In this sense, our union with the divine may begin with a sense of lack, but it will blossom into a gratitude-filled acknowledgement that we are already the fullness we seek.

Ameyn.

The Eastern Parallels:

Om purnam-adah purnam-idam
purnaat purnam-udacyate
purnasya purnam-aadaaya
purnam-eva-avashishyate

Translation: You are the fullness. There is fullness, here is
fullness. From the fullness, the fullness is born. Remove the
fullness and the fullness alone remains.

--Isa Upanishad

Going Deeper:

Breathe in, with compassion, that part of you that feels its
poverty, its separateness. Really acknowledge and feel it, the
poignant sense of aloneness that echoes there at times. Now,
breathe out to that density and loneliness a sense of spacious
connection, the smaller I AM held and continuous with the
larger I AM.

Summation:

**To Search means to unite and trust inner and outer experience
as lamps along the pathway of our already-present connection
with God.**

Logion 4

Yeshua says,

"A person of advanced age
must go immediately and
ask an infant born just
seven days ago about life's source.
Such asking leads to life
when what is first becomes last.
United, they become a single whole."

First Response:

All possible times and spaces touch fingertips-
advanced age and birth,
immediate and eternal,
verbal and non-verbal
first and last
all sliding together into unity,
into wholeness.

We ask, we search,
through the very lens of
paradox.

Today in Wisdom's Caravan:

As we begin to explore the act of searching, we are immediately brought into the presence of paradox with this logion—beginnings and endings, first and last, verbal and non-verbal are all at play, moving toward a recognition of their shared unity. Yeshua couches the truth in the simplest of motions, of going to the side of a baby and seeing the human face of the Beginning Time.

And yet, if we move out of the abstract and into a lived experience, we can see how a baby rests, its belly rising and falling effortlessly with the breath. If all is well with him or her, cries will be heard and responded to, needs will be met, arms will enfold and sweep the small bundle into the daily chores in a dance of gentle participation. For the infant, there is only now, but it is a deeply *relational* now. To see this, all that is required of us is simple attention to something small and quite unremarkable really. The seeing, though, also requires us to acknowledge the tremendous responsibility, respect and tenderness such an encounter evokes within us. Yeshua is not saying we should lose our discernment and be *like* an infant. Instead, he requires us to pay attention to the continuity between our beginning point and now, with our whole selves, heart and head.

To see this with attention also means we will begin to recognize how we ourselves expect to meet and be met by God in our search for union—that God who is ever at all the points in the caravan of life.

Ameyn.

The Eastern Parallels:

"The smile that flickers on the baby's lips when he sleeps—does anyone know where it was born? Yes there is a rumor that a pale beam of a crescent moon touched the edges of a vanishing autumn cloud and there the smile was first born in the dream of a dew-washed morning."

--Rabindranath Tagore

Going Deeper:

As you breathe out, feel as if you are a newborn held by the cosmos. As you breathe in, hold, in turn, the whole of that cosmos within yourself.

Summation:

To Search means we must be willing to transcend, with the vehicle of simple awareness, the words, roles, ages, genders and other markers of our culture in order to see the Beginning Point of our journey. And in that seeing, recognize our Self as well.

Logion 5

Yeshua says,

"Come to know the One
in the presence before you,
and everything hidden from you
will be revealed.
For there is nothing concealed
that will not be revealed,
and nothing buried
that will not be raised."

First Response:

It's there in a glance!
Eye to eye,
when black pupil meets black pupil
we see into the living void,
the holy breath still moving over the deep.
Before words come
all the worlds are there
and the suns as well,
wisdom and compassion
wed in
intimate relationship.

Today in Wisdom's Caravan:

Again, Yeshua beckons us to play with the paradox of the many and the one, two-ness of the presence before you and yet the basic unity that is there as well. The alchemy of relationship is based on a potent mix of wisdom and compassion, of relative reality and ultimate reality. Later, Yeshua will use metaphors of "eating" to describe this movement of spirit as two "objects" of matter, the eater and the eaten, become one.

He also stresses that because everything is "in unity through presence", nothing can be hidden, buried, or concealed. Unity must, by its very nature, incorporate all the secrets, the dark and the light, the obvious and the shadowed. One way to interpret the word "Allah" for instance is "everything we know about God" and "everything we do not know about God" in union. That union also includes all the hidden and shadowed parts of us, all of which, as the Sufis say, must "come to the table" and be included in everything that God is.

For the seeker this is good news indeed because the answer to our searching is already an integral part of us. It's not "will we find?" but in fact, *we cannot help but find* if we are mindful and aware. Our relationship with the multiplicity of life will illuminate all of life in its wholeness. Notice there is no struggle here, merely awareness that is a normal, if sometimes neglected, part of consciousness.

Ameyn.

The Eastern Parallels:

"Let us adore the Lord, the luminous One, who is in fire, who is in water, who is in plants and trees, who pervades the whole universe."

--Shvetashvatara Upanishad

Going Deeper:

On the in-breath, feel the skin that enfolds you. On the out-breath, feel as if you are sharing what is within you with everything beyond your skin. Then, as you breathe in again, feel all that wonder, mystery and life enter into you, held within

48

you. Breathe and stay in this place where the skin becomes thin and fine, in and out, hidden and apparent, all resting together as one.

Summation:

We will be successful in our Search. Indeed, it is inevitable that we shall find because nothing is truly hidden.

Logion 6

His students asked him,

"Do you want us to fast?
How shall we pray?
Should we give offerings?
From what food must we abstain?"

Yeshua answered,

"Stop lying.
Do not do what you hate
because everything here lies open
before heaven.
Nothing hidden remains secret,
for the veil will be stripped away from all
that lies concealed behind it."

First Response:

Bind me back to a time
when religion was not
another word for psychology;
when the shaman's journey
or the Christian Mass
told the story of relationship,
illuminated the ties that bound
life to life to
Mystery.

We work too hard now—
what does life mean?
How does the past haunt today?
Who are all these voices clamoring inside?
I wonder—

why not invite it all in and serve tea?
and afterwards,
gently,
walk the line between earth and water and sky,
hum a tune from childhood,
and recall
not one of us arose from independent nothingness.
Reweave yourself, but intuitively,
in the meal served,
in the hat knitted and passed on,
in the laughter in the grocery check-out line.
If sin is simply that which is "unripe",
then explode with flavor, with juice,
or if it is time,
with a fearless releasing to earth.
Live interwoven with it all,
and tell me
where you can really fall?

Today in Wisdom's Caravan:

I am always struck by the disciples' underlying sense of anxiety and fear in this saying. They so want to know that they are doing things "right", as though by mimicking the behaviors of religious observance, they can feel like they are correct, accepted and loved. They focus on their own wills, and on their own "spiritual effort" that is wholly based in the outward show and behaviors of religious etiquette. There is very little sense here that actions must take place from the inside out, or that the feeling of devotion precedes the attempt to express that emotion through action.

The most startling thing for us to see today is that Yeshua is trying hard to convey a radical and attainable freedom. He wants his disciples to know that the grade book *they* are trying to construct presupposes a grade will be given, and the one who bestows that mark may be very formidable indeed. Yeshua is attempting to release his students from both that fear and their narrow brand of thinking, showing them that the "hidden" God as well as the shadowy and judgmental sides of his disciples, are not veiled at all. There can be no true relationship in a power-over way of belief or living. The lie that we tell ourselves is that there *is* a judge; that we can linger behind behaviors that have no basis in the very truth that is the core of ourselves. We are called to so much more than this.

We will be noticing throughout the Gospel of Thomas that "heaven" is not located anywhere other than in our own state of consciousness. So again, when Yeshua says that "everything here lies open to heaven", he is pointing to the inner awareness that is the basis of a true relationship with others and the divine.

Ameyn.

The Eastern Parallels:

"He who offers Me with devotion a leaf, a flower, a fruit, a cup of water, that offering of love from the earnest soul is acceptable to me."

--The Bhagavad-Gita

Going Deeper:

Go outside into your yard or garden, or find someplace inside that you can set designate as a small sacred space. Allow yourself to create a simple offering that captures the tenor of your relationship with God. Feel the connection before you act, as if "that which you are seeking is causing you to seek" or "what you seek is seeking you" (Rumi).

Summation:

A successful Search does not require outward behaviors, but rather, an inward change of consciousness.

Logion 7

Yeshua says,

"A lion eaten by a man is blessed
as it changes to human form,
but a human devoured by a lion is cursed
as lion becomes human."

First Response:

Have you eaten rage in that cold place,
hoping
for a little warmth between your ribs
and found instead
how it binds
your fists,
wrinkles the skin between your eyes,
lifts your shoulders to your ears?
And woe if you try to speak out of a stomach full like that.
It is not enough to swallow fury;
we must invite it to the table within
and sit it down,
tip our head and listen
so it may settle into our bones—
a more civilized beast
holding up the mirror of life to our own faces.

Today in Wisdom's Caravan:

We are creatures of many faces, some of them
convenient masks, others instinctual reactions to our
environment. We have good control over some of these
"selves", others, not so much. The movement toward
relationship requires coming to our inner table with

consciousness and "dining" with the shadowy, the violent, the unloved parts of us. The transformation that Yeshua has named as "eating" is quite profound—a deep integration of those parts of ourselves that, while perhaps part of our natural ecology, can also cause harm if left unexamined. The search must take us into these corners and dark places if we are to be whole—and it is only in a state of wholeness that we can meet and fully interact with all the other pieces of this magnificent creation.

The humans who are consumed by these shadow aspects of themselves will not be able to meet the world in wholeness. Even if "the lion" is kept carefully hidden, its effects will accumulate in bodily tension, in cynicism, and in impatience or irritability. Our own psychologists have told us that repression will "out" in the end. Again, what Yeshua is doing is something more radical than turning us away from the parts we don't wish to own—he's calling us to "eat", just like at the communion table, to experience an intimately transformative inner event that will allow us to enter more fully into community and relationship with others beyond this thin layer of skin.

Ameyn.

The Eastern Parallels:

"The evolution of nature is the modification of the soul. The soul in essence is the same in all forms of being. Its' expression is modified by the body. The unity of soul, this common substance of humanity, is the basis of ethics and morality. In this sense, all are one, and to hurt one's brother is to hurt one's Self. Love is simply an expression of this infinite unity. Upon what dualistic system can you explain love?"

--Swami Vivekananda

Going Deeper:

Next time you feel yourself "being eaten by the lion" – feeling anger, jealousy, rage, entitlement and the like—watch carefully what the emotion and action feels like and see if you can find the trigger that caused it to arise. Can you recall the feeling-mind before the actual physical response? Try to sit with these shadows face to face in your imagination, and as you breathe in, let them fill you. As you breathe out, welcome them with patience and kindness. How does this change the texture of the states themselves? Notice this is not repression or turning away, but embracing in love and compassion our wild and seemingly dangerous selves.

Summation:

To Search means all the pieces of us must come to the Holy Communion table within.

Logion 8

Yeshua says,

"A true human being can be compared to a wise fisherman
who casts his net into the sea and draws it
up from below,
full of small fish.
Hidden among them is one larger,
exceptional fish that
he seizes immediately,
throwing back all the rest
without a second thought.
Whoever has ears
let them understand this."

First Response:
Laundry, dirty dishes, dusting
paint the kitchen,
facebook, blog, email
walk, swim, bike...
the choices flash like sun on night-crawler skin,
each valid, each
demanding and wriggling in the
corner of my eye.
Lord, send me that one fat snowflake.
Let it perch on the tip of my glove
reminding me
that a single moment of seeing
truly
re-arranges everything in crystalline perspective.

Today in Wisdom's Caravan:

We have become a culture hooked on little fishes. I remember the lines of an REM song—"Crazy what you could have had"—and cringe a little when I look around at my own house, filled with all that delights. Books in stacks. Songs by the thousands on the Cloud Drive. Animals. Mismatched but clung-to dishes. Closets full of old clothes. Statues. Plants. Tiny model armies on six bookcases. I'm not hoarding by the psychological definition but when I start to take stock, I'm a little embarrassed by the richness and all the ways my attention can be shattered.

All of it can become the astounding variety that binds.

This goes far beyond the material, though. We sag under the little fishes of entertainment, of social "to-dos", the pressure of the "networks" we are expected to maintain, the "must-dos" of the voices in our own heads, creating lists and agendas and timetables. Even Yeshua understood that in the midst of something mundane like work, the big fish may show up and in that instant, reorder everything in us from the act of eating to the source of our livelihoods, from how we prioritize our lives to how we strive to be more present and faithful to the jewel of pure consciousness.

He asks us here to enter into the practice of discernment, to create a state of mind that allows us to recognize the big fish when it comes up out of the deep and then to take action, throwing the rest of the little fishes back into the sea. The action is not done with a sense of loss, asceticism or regret, but with the overwhelming wonder of a searcher who has finally *found*.

Ameyn.

The Eastern Parallels:

"Take up one idea. Make that one idea your life; dream of it; think of it; live on that idea. Let the brain, the body, the muscles, nerves, every part of your body be full of that idea and just leave every other idea alone. This is the way to success and this is the way great spiritual giants are produced."

--Swami Vivekananda

Going Deeper:

Take up your journal today and draw or note the central image or idea of your personal "one big fish". How does your life reflect this focus, intent, calling or idea? How might you craft a personal practice that reminds you to throw the small fish back into the sea?

Summation:

To Search requires a process of discernment, ordering our lives around the big and possibly paradigm-changing intuition that arises within us.

Logion 9

Yeshua says,

"A farmer went out to plant,
seed in hand he scattered
it everywhere.
Some fell on the surface of the road.
Birds came and ate it.
Others fell on rocky ground
and could not take root in the earth,
or send grain heavenward,
so it never germinated.
Still other seeds fell among
weeds and brambles which choked it
and insects devoured it.
Some, however, fell onto fertile soil
which produced fruit of high quality
yielding in the heavens as much as sixty
and one-hundred and twenty percent."

First Response:

The nuthatch perches on the squirrel-proof feeder
(although my squirrels didn't read the blurb about that)
flinging seeds in a spray of glistening black and tan.
He pauses,
flips his tail at my study window,
and dives in again.
Presently they come:
the spotted towhee,
the dark eyed junco,
and a single dark-headed grosbeak,
the ground feeders who vacuum up and take away
the kernel on the wing,
let the husks separate and settle

as new compost
into the warm mud.

Today in Wisdom's Caravan:

I was just speaking to a friend the other day about casting seeds in the form of ideas—how we are never sure where our words might land and how they might one day take a form we could never anticipate. And not just our words, but also, how we act and move and the choices we make—everything is observed, noted by the deepest parts of our minds and, often, by the beloved community we walk with.

It's a sobering and delightful practice, to be as generous as the nuthatch and the sower above with our wisdom and our foibles, to seed our relationships with the wild abandon of sharing ourselves without masks and with a comfortable transparency. Sometimes when we look at the lopsided plant our actions and words produce, we can only stare into the mirror it holds up to our faces.

This is the bread of life, you see, baked from the grains we share with others, seeded down into conversations and lovemaking, in grocery lines and social protests, in yoga classes and dirty dishes. There is a single flavor in it all if you can catch it as Yeshua obviously hopes you will.

Ameyn.

The Eastern Parallels:

"Ask nothing, want nothing in return. Give what you have to give; it will come back to you, but do not think of that now."

"Each work has to pass through these stages—ridicule, opposition and then acceptance. Those who think ahead of their time will be misunderstood."

"A few heart-whole, sincere and energetic men and women can do more in a year than a mob in a century."

--Swami Vivekananda

Going Deeper:

What seeds have you scattered today? Take a little time to name some of them for yourself—the smile you gave to the gas station clerk, the coffee and chocolate you offered to a hurting friend, the birdfeeder you filled in the winter, the partner you listened to. These are the little seeds we scatter through our day. Some will give you back 120% some time, but you might not be aware of those plants growing at all right now.

Summation:

Searching means nurturing what we are able, both the seeds of wisdom we receive and those we, in turn, sow.

Logion 10

Yeshua says,

*"See! I have sown fire into
the cosmos and I shall guard it carefully
until it blazes."*

First Response:

In the new heat I worked,
fire again in limbs too still for too long
drawing up light with the in-breath,
grounded and steady as I breathed out,
my eyes watching the rain
but gesturing warmth,
transformation,
awareness,
the living energies of creation.
We must blaze,
our actions alchemical,
our thoughts,
seedlings lifting sunward,
our lives,
hearth-fires
one to another.

Today in Wisdom's Caravan:

Today, I wish I could just keep going in the poetic vein. I can get away with words like "alchemical" and "blazing" there. Prose wants a steadier and more reasonable hand. And yet, this tension between the freer verse and the constraints of the ordered paragraph captures the intent behind Yeshua's words beautifully. For fire is both the destroyer and the creator, that which lights or blinds, that which digests our meals or lets this house stand while it consumes another. It all depends on how it is used, just as knowledge without discernment and action without forethought can injure.

Fire is scattered through the universe by our own hands; indeed, each thing we touch, think about, interact with can either burn or heal. The energy of creation is brilliant, hot, ever moving, bringing forth change, and we dance with that always. The spiritual path, then, is an awareness of this fact, well-seeded with wonder and awe. *We are called to play with fire!* Otherwise, we are the dry stick that will simply be burned, the cold hearth that cannot welcome the friend, the bored couch potato merely taking in entertainment without real digestion and growth. This is the fire of devotion we are called to—the light of awareness, heat of transformation and the energy that transcends every vessel that tries to hold it in a steady state.

Ameyn.

The Eastern Parallels:

"All power is within you. You can do anything and everything. Believe in that. Do not believe you are weak; do not believe you are half-crazy lunatics, as most of us do nowadays. Stand up and express the divinity within you."

"Come out into the broad light of day, come out of the little narrow path, for how can the infinite soul rest content to live and die in small ruts?"

"Come out into the universe of light. Everything in the universe is yours, stretch out your arms and embrace it with love. If you ever felt you wanted to do that, you have felt God."

--Swami Vivekananda

Going Deeper:

Rub your hands together briskly for a moment, and then place them over your eyes. Now, let that activity and heat sink in during this time of stillness. How is this exercise like the idea that "fire is seeded into the cosmos?" Allow yourself to explore the metaphor in poetry, prose or art.

Summation:

To Search is to look deeply into the fire of the cosmos—the movement, transformation, and process that is I AM.

Logion 11

Yeshua says,

"The sky and all that lies in the
dimensions above it will cease to exist.
The dead know nothing of life,
and the living will never die.
When you consume that which is already
dead, you are turning it back into life.
So, then, when you, too, emerge
back into the Light,
what will you do?
For on the day when you were created one
you also became two,
but when you come to realize your
twoness again,
what will you do?"

First Response:

Along the single stem of the fern,
the flat, elongated leaves pair up,
marching down the spine to the tiniest
singular tip,
a triangular tongue sipping the breeze.
Out of the riled waves,
a rare gray whale breaches
and falls into mystery again.
The dead mouse eaten by the chicken,
who in turn,
lays my breakfast—see it now?
Two-one, two-one,
like breathing,
like warmth and fire.

Today in Wisdom's Caravan:

In many ways, the Gospel of Thomas challenges our rational and linear minds. Notice how the above logion links together seemingly disparate statements? But when we shift our lens a little and read it as poetry, then the meaning that resonates between the statements becomes a great deal more interesting and clear. This shift, the ability to read metaphorically, is the challenge and delight of working with this particular scripture. By its very construction, it asks us to practice the twoness-within-oneness that Yeshua is trying to convey. Our binary minds like to dance with "either/ors" rather than the more global "both/ands".

Death and life seem like two, but through the singular act of transformation (eating for instance, burning with fire for another), they are united. Who is the eater and who the eaten? Isn't the fire also the thing burned? The process is truly like breathing; one beat, the air exists outside of us and yet with the next inhale, that air and our bodies become one. We exhale our singular selves back into the world where it breaks into manyness again, food for plants now, mixing with the breath of others, the two and the one blurring. Everything is simply energy exchanges, held in stillness only for a heartbeat in our awareness.

The God that Yeshua points to here is not *a being* at all— it is simply **BEING** itself and it is not just stillness! It is the very movement of life. To enter into an understanding of that life, to find the Kingdom around and within us (one, two, can you catch it here?), we have to pay attention and transcend *preferring* one way of looking to another. The Way of Yeshua is just this easy and just this difficult.

Ameyn.

The Eastern Parallels:

"I Am the thread that runs through all these pearls"...such are the different [parts of relative reality] and God is the thread that runs through all of them; most people, however, are entirely unconscious of it."

--Swami Vivekananda

"The sacrifice Itself is the spirit. Spirit and oblation are one. It is the spirit Itself which is sacrificed in Its own fire."

--The Bhagavad-Gita

Going Deeper:

First, find a pencil. Look at it carefully in its entirety. Then, notice how you can hold your gaze and attention on just the eraser. Breathe for a while, really seeing this one thing. Notice, then, that the eraser itself begins to separate into pixels of light and dark, smudges, as well as damaged areas puckering the smoothness. Can you begin to see that oneness and twoness are conventions of language and where we place our attention rather than Reality as such?

Summation:

To Search means to pay attention to the breath-like dance of the two and the one, finally asking what is the movement of those distinctions Itself?

Logion 12

His students said,

"We know we cannot hold onto you,
so who will lead us then?"

Yeshua said,

"Wherever you find yourselves,
turn to James, one of the Just,
for whom heaven and earth
have come into being."

First Response:

James the Just—
did you know a Bishop would name himself after you
and
I think I can hear a haunting laugh in the cosmos—
the hidden trickster,
who plays so ably with words,
who has convinced the smoky-eyed and needy to
believe you
are one
of the successors of Yeshua.

As if words, ideas and institutions
could contain fire.

As if being led is the same
as holding our hands to living flame
warming or even burning ourselves
moth-like in Light.

Are we not asked, demanded even,

to stand?
Those who have ears,
I hope they heard
all those years ago
and smiled.

Today in Wisdom's Caravan:

For a long time, this logion contained very little meaning for me. There were shadowy aspects of the twin here, as well as the obvious sense of Yeshua calming the fears of his disciples. That was sort of sweet in its own way, but I always felt that I was missing something important.

But then the title struck me: James the Just. As in justice and law, that intellect that separates the universe into dos and don'ts and into rights and wrongs. It is that leaning that divides heaven from earth, making them come into being although such a division is illusion in its best dress.

Sometimes, when we search, we want very much to be led, to know we are on the "right" path, protected and "justified." That is the role that both poor gurus and some institutional religions slip into, slyly or innocently giving us the leadership we so desperately want at the cost of our own personal sovereignty.

The search is sometimes a lonely and frightening state to be in. It's natural that the disciples who were deeply in love with their Master would try to secure ways to go on without him. But over and over again, Yeshua is trying to teach them that they must not look *at* him, but rather, become *like* him, in union with the divine. It is a state of being he will call "standing" later in this text and it resonates through all the logia. Only when we stand does the search begin to shift into finding and all that comes after that moment. Ameyn.

70

The Eastern Parallels:

"On one still morning, the Buddha gathered his disciples and pulled from his robe a single lotus flower. He did not speak, but simply held it up, his eyes scanning the crowd. And they fell into conversation, expounding on the meaning of the flower, its symbolism, and how it fit into all the teachings of the Buddha.

But one disciple, Mahakasyapa, simply looked into those wise eyes and smiled broadly.

Buddha smiled back. "Everything I can give, I have given to Mahakasyapa," he announced.

Mahakasyapa became the Buddha's successor on that day."

--The Flower Sermon

Going Deeper:

We are slowly becoming a Christian culture that is learning to see into the depths of our traditional texts in a way that is not strictly literal. That's useful because The Gospel of Thomas requires us to shift our view, putting on reading lenses that hold relative and ultimate reality in a glance, a kind of bifocal awareness. Today, go to any verse at random in your favorite scripture or piece of literature or poetry. First, read the lines aloud and simply hear them. Then, after a bit of clearing silence, read them aloud again. This time ask, "what are these words saying to me beneath the literal interpretation?" Finally, after a bit more silence, allow yourself to settle on just one word or very short phrase that seems particularly important for you today. Hold that phrase and enter into at least ten minutes of silence with it before you offer up a gentle thank-you for the gift of insight and time of peace.

Summation:

To Search, we must not cling to institutions, teachers, or books, but recognize the fire of the cosmos within us as our greatest authority.

Logion 13

Yeshua asked his students,
"Tell me, who am I like?
To whom do you compare me?"

Simon Peter said,
"You are just like an angel."
Matthew said,
"You are a philosopher of wisdom."
Thomas said,
"Master, I cannot find words to express who you
really are."

Yeshua said,
"Thomas, it is no longer necessary
for me to be your Master
for you are drinking from the gushing spring I
have opened for you,
and you have become intoxicated."

Then Yeshua took Thomas aside and spoke
three sayings to him in private.
When Thomas returned to the company
of his companions they, of course, asked him,
"What did Yeshua say to you?"

"If I were to tell you even one of the things
he spoke to me," Thomas replied,
"you would pick up these rocks
and stone me
and then
fire would blaze out of them and
burn you."

First Response:

Name an object
and you think you know it.
Name a person,
and the same thing happens.
Conflate object and person
and you'll reap misery a hundred fold.
Pass on Mystery with words? Good luck!
The little mystery of communication
tangles on itself while
the greater Mystery
shakes such dust from its feet,
reaches out to help the neighbor,
drinks the wine and eats at your table.
And when you see the Mystery then,
just out of the corner of your eye
where words cannot quite reach,
then you will begin to light up--
the next Big Bang already in motion.

Today in Wisdom's Caravan:

This logion calls to mind the Transfiguration story in the Bible, without all the fireworks of course. I've always liked these words, the way they point us past objectification of a human being into the heart of seeing all the divinity moving around us. We cage our world in words and think we know it. We feel the urge to build altars and temples, trying through action to come into relationship with it all.

But true relationship is not about *doing*, it is about *being* and responding to *Reality As Such*.

The only way the disciples can move from being students to walking fully with Yeshua is to see beyond his human form and their own, to get past the mythological metaphors and safe intellectual constructs. Only when they are able to do so will they partake in the same light and life that Yeshua embodies.

Our search, then must take us past the labels we apply, the words we use, the concepts that make us feel like we have ground beneath our feet. Yeshua is challenging us to go deeper, to see without thinking we know. That groundlessness, that *not knowing*, is the beginning of finding.

Ameyn.

The Eastern Parallels:

"Swamiji, what is Vedanta, please?" I began.

He (Vivekananda) answered in his firm, soft voice, "Vedanta is the essential philosophy original to the Hindus, but we claim it is the essential philosophy of all religions. The major ideas of Vedanta are, first, the ultimate existence. We hold all the things we see around us are ultimately reducible to one substance. Normally, in every philosophical system, there will be three main questions: What is the nature of man? What is the nature of God as Ultimate reality? What is the nature of nature?

Different religious systems and different philosophical systems have different answers. Vedanta, especially non-dualistic Vedanta—Advaita as it is called, say that all three are one. Man in his ultimate nature, nature in its ultimate nature and God in his ultimate nature are the same. This is the basic position of Vedanta."

--Swami Swahananda

Going Deeper:

Lay out three objects on a surface. First, simply name them: match, cup, spoon for instance.

Then, pretend you have never seen such things before, that they have no names, no assigned roles to play in daily living. They are mysterious and ancient pieces, and you are gazing at them for the very first time.

How does this experience change how you interact with "objective" reality?

Summation:

To Search means we must leave our comfortable words, concepts, and personal mythological systems behind so that we are open enough to find.

Logion 14

Yeshua says

"If you fast you will only be giving birth
to sin in yourself.
If you pray,
your prayers will come back
to haunt you.
If you give to charity,
you will create evil
within your own spirit.

If, however, you travel through
a region and they welcome you,
eat what is put in front of you,
and heal their sick.
For it is not what goes into your mouth
that contaminates you,
but what comes out of it".

First Response:

Imagine
never seeing an image of yourself
(and already you can catch the pun)
just the occasional laugh,
the feathered kiss
or rib-creaking hug,
the spoon touching your lips
the water, cool and swallowed gratefully on a hot day,
the earth damp and black under your fingertips,
the drum-beat under your breastbone,
the smell of the lily-of-the-valley,
the stars overhead

when the world presses itself away
in shadows.

Where is the "you" in all of this?

Simply everywhere, my friend.

Today in Wisdom's Caravan:

Often the logia of the Gospel of Thomas are compared with Zen Buddhist koans. Our attention fixes on one part of the saying and then, Yeshua flips both it and our minds in an Aikido-like ballet of illogic. Those moments are precious, really; they trigger the inherent plasticity in our brains that not only hold a mirror up to our inner selves, but also make us laugh out-loud with the slippery and mysterious energy of spoken communication.

The trouble with prayer, fasting, and alms-giving is not located in the acts themselves, but in the intellectual and egoic games we play with such "religiously" expected activities. Yeshua is asking, in a very real sense, "who does these things and why?" Where does the motivation arise—from an outside expectation of "right behavior or from the heart's longing for honest relationship? How are the actions performed? With a sense of listening for the cheer of the crowd, the approval of peers or with a profoundly secret need to see the face of the Beloved?

True relational rituals are simple—break bread in thankfulness, interact with care, heal who and what you can, practice gentle speech. In other words, love thy neighbor as thyself because the loving is the very essence of true religious practice.

Ameyn.

The Eastern Parallels:

"Desire, want, is the father of all misery. Desires are bound by the laws of success and failure. Desires must bring misery. The great secret of true success, of true happiness, is this: the person who asks for no return, the perfectly unselfish person, is the most successful."

"First, believe in the world—there is meaning behind everything."

"Books are infinite in number and time is short. The secret of knowledge is to take what is essential. Take that and try to live up to it."

--Swami Vivekananda

Going Deeper:

Think a moment about the spiritual practices you do—perhaps holy reading, meditation or prayer, ritual and church observances, etc. When did you begin these things and for what reason? Has that motivation changed over time? What activities that seem compulsory, as arising from outside yourself, could be released? Are there activities that might better express your soul and your relationship with the Divine at this time in your life? Explain.

Summation:

To Search means to be courageous enough to shake off the dust of traditional or expected religious actions in favor of entering into a loving relationship with the world.
Logion 15

Yeshua says,

*"When the time comes
and you are able to look upon the
Unborn One,
fall prostrate in worship,
for you have found your own true Father,
(your Source and Origin) at last."*

First Response:

Abba I have called you
those times when I needed a compass,
a listening ear.
It wasn't wrong, to name you thus,
to cry "daddy" to the universe
and feel the sense of being
carried, held and heard.
But sometimes
Abba teases apart in the wild wind
dancing the fir trees,
or
gets lost in the script
of the stars,
flung out thin and broad.
The secret beyond the name?

This silent lump in my heart and throat
is
still
holy.

Today in Wisdom's Caravan:

When the search begins to give us glints and glimpses of the enormity of the Mystery we are pursuing, our words leave us and then, our bodies drop into the deepest attitude of prayer in awe. I do mean the word awe here—wonder mixed with a healthy dose of fear as our egos face up and out and understand their ephemeral nature at last.

The emotional reaction as we face our own vast beginning place is normal and good. We feel the deep relationship with Ultimate Reality, the truest parent of all parents, the conflation of beginning and ending points that guide us toward something more than merely relative reality. This kind of experience keeps us going, lifts and puts bounce into our steps as we begin to truly find.

Ameyn.

The Eastern Parallels:

"All that is real in me is God; all that is real in God is I. The gulf between God and human beings is thus bridged. Thus we find how, by knowing God, we find the kingdom of heaven within us."

--Swami Vivekananda

"Be not afraid, be not bewildered, on seeing this terrific form of Mine. Free from fear and glad of heart, recall again my other form. (Krishna addresses his friend and student Arjuna after showing him the full extent of his divine manifestation. Arjuna, a peerless warrior, is dropped to his knees in awe.)"

--Bhagavad-Gita

Going Deeper:

Come to your knees if you are able, then fold down over them into child's pose or lay outstretched on the floor, face down, your arms out to your sides in the shape of a cross. Notice how you feel—there may be many textures in this posture of surrender. Feel the vast infinite holding you, participating with you in this surrender. Later, share with others or in your art or journal or music what you discovered about yourself and God.

Summation:

To Search means finding the bravery to look into the vast Reality that is the womb from which we've truly sprung.

Logion 16

Yeshua says,

"Some of you are thinking
perhaps I have come into the cosmos
to bring it peace.
No!
You do not yet realize
that I have come to throw it
into utter chaos
through burning, blade and battle.
Five will be living in one household.
Three will face off against two
and two against three.
Parents will rise up against children,
and children against their parents,
until at last they shall stand united
on their own feet."

First Response:

The mirror lies my friend—
you see one face but already you are pretending to be two,
the seer and the seen,
face to face.
You can't confront the inside by always looking outward.
And if you could peel back that furrowed brow,
no frame could hold your many reflections then.
Maybe better to simply shut your eyes and hear them,
the should-look-likes,
the opinions,
the expectations
swirling
and
where did they all arise?

You threw open all the windows and doors in your house, and
they flooded in.
A first, they promised to remodel and repaint,
fix the squeaks,
carpet the living-room floor
but you let them move in,
not happily perhaps,
but still, you fed them, each one.
Sit here quietly beside Me for a moment.
Let Me be your mirror
just for these few breaths
and tell you,
there is a still small voice under all that hubbub.
Can you heed it?
With this single, standing reflection
can you simply recall
being
One?

Today in Wisdom's Caravan:

I think Cynthia Bourgeault was right when she
commented that most of us have been schooled in the idea that
Jesus was "nice". And yet, throughout the Gospel of Thomas,
Yeshua stands both firm and implacable. We must discern
truth, teasing it out from the fictional constructs of our inner
lives. That requires a clear identification of those voices living
under the roof of our scalp who no longer serve us. Children
and parents, friends and relations, powerful strangers and
religious authorities all try to "help" us in our spiritual journey
by framing our lives with templates of their own. It's not meant
to be mean-spirited; in fact, many of those voices rattling
around in our head were put there because we loved and
listened to them, or were offered to us because we were indeed
cherished.

But Yeshua is telling us in no uncertain terms that at some point in our work, we must stand up, our head touching the sky and our feet upheld by the ground and realize our own unique, valid and fire-tested being. Unless we get to our own feet, and as the Buddha once said, "see the house-builder, the illusion maker, the voices of propriety" we will never mature into a kind of person who is whole. We will be the fuzzy image of someone else's encounter with the divine.

And that does not just weaken you, it also compromises one unique facet in the incredibly complex and beautiful jewel that is Reality. Each of us must stand up and face the Divine fully naked and as ourselves, because only in that basic unity will we begin to see our union and participation within THAT which is the greatest Truth and ground of our very being.

Ameyn.

The Eastern Parallels:

"If you see the Buddha on the road, kill him."

--Zen Saying

Going Deeper:

When you look at your own daily choices, beliefs, habits and ideas, can you trace any of them back to an actual experience or were they instilled in you by another? Do they serve you today? How might you begin to stand as Yeshua asks, letting go of what no longer vibrates with the energy of your breathing relationship with Mystery?

Summation:

To Search means to listen for the still, small voice of a greater unity beneath the cacophony of imposed opinions, rules, and institutional dogmas.

Logion 17

Yeshua says,

"What your own eyes cannot see,
your human ears
do not hear,
your physical hands cannot touch,
and what is inconceivable to the human
mind—that I will give to you."

The First Response:

Let the out-breath go,
pushing your skin large,
breaking the connection between
brain and
eye
and
ear,
where the tangle of the blackberry bush,
finally loses its thorns,
where the water warms then dissipates at your touch,
where even the swirl of galaxies cannot hold you
and yet, you can still dwell
as a small brilliant flame
in your sweet beating heart.

Today in Wisdom's Caravan:

Yeshua relentlessly calls us throughout this Gospel to be bigger than our own precious skins, to transcend the grasping and often fallible ownership of our senses, to begin to find a touchstone in the metaphoric and spacious world. Other logia will balance this seeming other worldliness, asking us to begin to recognize that peace of heart and mind will require of us an ability to bring together both relative and ultimate reality. In other words, we will be challenged to move in *this* world, but with the understanding that there is a deeper layer providing its foundation and ultimately, its meaning.

This logion, too, might be looked at as a call into a different kind of relationship with not just our bodies and world, but with the other beings who we "interpenetrate" with every act of breathing, seeing, touching. We are so much larger that our own skins, and often it is in community that we begin to practice the skills of compassion and empathy—of recognizing the oneness beneath the many-ness and the unity beneath seeming duality. Watch for other logia that will begin to expand upon this theme.

When we get beyond "our" bodies and minds, we will encounter a spaciousness that can inform the way we approach problems, interactions with others and with the many faces of our inner world. In a sense, it is the ultimate way to put all the challenges and joys of life into perspective, catching the silence between the in-breath of self and the out-breath of annihilation. This is the very home of the still small voice, reconciling opposites into union and yet always dynamic.

Ameyn.

The Eastern Parallels:

"Know the Self to be sitting in the chariot, the body to be the chariot, the intellect (*buddhi*) the charioteer, and the mind the reins. The senses they call the horses, the objects of the senses are their roads. When he (the Highest Self) is in union with the body, the senses, and the mind, then wise people call him the Enjoyer."

--Katha Upanishad

"As large as this ether (all space) is, so large is that ether within the heart. Both heaven and earth are contained within it, both fire and air, both sun and moon, both lightning and stars; and whatever there is of him (the Self) here in the world, and whatever is not (i. e. whatever has been or will be), all that is contained within it."

--Chandogya Upanishad

"That which is not uttered by speech, that by which the word is expressed, know That alone to be Brahman, and not this (non-Brahman) which is being worshipped. That which one does not think with the mind, that by which, they say, the mind is thought, know That alone to be Brahman, and not this (non-Brahman) which is being worshipped. That which man does not see with the eye, that by which man sees the activities of the eye, know That alone to be Brahman, and not this (non-Brahman) which is being worshipped. That which man does not hear with the ear, that by which man hears the ear's hearing, know That alone to be Brahman, and not this (non-Brahman) which is being worshipped. That which man does not smell with the organ of smell, that by which the organ of smell is attracted towards its objects, know That alone to be Brahman, and not this (non-Brahman) which is being worshipped."

--Kena Upanishad

Going Deeper:

Sit for a time, breathing deeply in and out. Then, on a mindful exhale, imagine yourself expanding out to the limits of your imagination. Hold there and inhale, then exhale and make yourself bigger still. Continue this until you feel impossibly large. Then, out-breath by out-breath, bring yourself back and back until your mind can rest in the center of your heart like a small flame of consciousness. Feel what it is like to be both vast and small, bound by senses and then unbound even by this earth. How will this kind of "knowing" affect your relationship with yourself and others?

Summation:

To Search means to begin to be willing to explore the intuitive realms that our senses and dualistically-conditioned thought processes cannot perceive on their own.

Logion 18

His students said to him,

"So tell us, then,
what our end and
destiny will be?"

Yeshua answered,

"have you already discovered
your origin so that now
you are free to seek after your end?
It is only at your source
that you will find your destiny.
Blessed are those who come to stand in their
place of origination,
for it is there that they will know their end—
never tasting death."

The First Response:

Spin these cycles round again,
the seed to plant to seed,
the egg to hen to egg,
the nut to tree to nut,
and when your mind reaches out
to stop that glorious
spiraling
creative
breathing of the universe,
remember
fence lines and
walls

lines of words
and moats of thought,
all must one day swirl away
in stardust.
Endings are for those
who are a little afraid
of
their
beginnings...
so
spin these cycles round again
and this time
laugh
out-loud.

Today in Wisdom's Caravan:

As a fiction writer, I am often called to simply trust that in its beginning place the novel is already full and complete—that the story will find a kind of end, but that end will also point the way forward into the next creative act. I believe that when a new reader takes up my "finished" book, the writer's energy is passed forward and inward both. Ending is a beginning and individuals enter into communication and communion. That's why reviews are often so difficult to read and sometimes write—they are an intimate reaction to an act of creative intimacy, and each will be generative in its own way.

The manifest form does *seem* to fall away—perhaps we eat the seed, crack open the egg or nut mentioned in the poem above, and yet, it becomes us then, still energy moving and dancing and not really ending. Our job as spiritual beings is to be able to hold the lines of tension between the apparent or perceived "end" and the continuance and twisting spirals of life. This is not the binary mind at work, with its yes/no, right/wrong/, dark/light ways of coming to the world. It is the deeper act of discernment, of comfort with chaos, of a love affair with ambiguity. This is the life-giving dance that assures us that while form falls away, there is THAT which will always start again, everlasting.

Ameyn.

The Eastern Parallels:

"All differences in this world are of degree, and not of kind, because oneness is the secret of everything."

— Swami Vivekananda

"Desire, ignorance, and inequality—this is the trinity of bondage."

— Swami Vivekananda

"The Self-Being pierced the openings outward; hence one looks outward, not within himself. A wise man looked towards the Self with reverted sight, seeking deathlessness. Children seek after outward desires; they come to the net of widespread death. But the wise, beholding deathlessness, seek not for the enduring among unenduring things."

--Katha Upanishad

Going Deeper:

Take time to list the apparent play of opposites in your life— eating/fasting, sleeping/waking, working/playing, planting/sowing in all its forms. Now look carefully at the list and see if you can find when this activity really begins or ends. Do you notice that each play of opposites, even "death" and "life", are simply mind-made designations breaking up a smooth, continuous sense of existence? So what really ends? Or really begins for that matter?

Summation:

To Search and begin to Find means to become conscious of the breaking down of opposites, even the great "opposites" of life and death.

Transition Logion 19

Yeshua says,

"Blessed are all who come
to live at the point of arising,
their 'genesis',
before they came into temporality.

If you become my students,
listening deeply to my words,
even these stones will serve you.

And in paradise
five evergreen trees await you.
They do not change in summer
nor shed their leaves in winter.
If you come to know them,
you will not know the taste of death."

The First Response:

Gates shall open for you;
there are no locks here.
The passage way between lies
narrow, focused,
the fossils in the stone path beneath your feet,
breathing still.
Can you swim as they do
in a salt sea of brilliant red?

And beyond, in the garden of paradise,
five evergreens sway, waiting.
Shall I name these five now?
Their roots like dendrites,

their branches like networks in your lungs?
This one, the eye,
capable of seeing everything in that first glance,
that one, the ear,
picking up pure vibration,
here one called touch,
feathering its needles in the wind,
over there,
the nose,
sniffing without regard both the sweet and the fire
and now,
this last,
tasting it all and finding it
good,
very good
indeed.

Today in Wisdom's Caravan:

To be present at our beginning place, before our slide
into the material world, requires of us a shift of consciousness
into the Now, which connects both past and future. Here we
are deathless, fearless, wide awake and functioning with all our
senses but in a way that is "evergreen". We just experience the
world with a perfect one-pointed attention. We will see, hear,
smell, taste and touch just what IS instead of what we expect or
wish, think we know, or try to avoid.

That re-entry into the paradise that is truthfully always
with us opens our senses wide. There is no naming here, no
breaking the world into numbers and knowable bits of data.
Because such a state was never "born", it also never "dies"; it is
the experience of pure conscious abiding, where both self-will
and grace become a singular action of attention. It is the
Kingdom and the Garden, entered through the narrow gate but
as I said in the poem, the entry point is never locked to us.

Each one of our senses, too, can be that gate. I picked up a stone at the beach today, black basalt shot through with white lines, and it took me back to my genesis and forward into that paradise state—smell of salt, touch of cool rock, the black and white colors weaving together, the sound of the waves beside me, the taste of old seaweed on my tongue. Past, present and future, entered all at once, through the gates of my senses. And it was very, very good.

Ameyn.

The Eastern Parallels:

"There is neither Self-knowledge nor Self-perception to those whose senses are not under control. Without Self-perception there is no peace; and without peace there can be no happiness."

--The Bhagavad-Gita

"One who has control over the mind is tranquil in heat and cold, in pleasure and pain, and in honor and dishonor; and is ever steadfast with the Supreme Self."

--The Bhagavad-Gita

"Every step I take in Light is mine forever."
--Swami Vivekananda

Going Deeper:

Look out your window right now and really see it without editing or expectation. When you do this, what happens to the colors, the textures, the blend of lawn, sky, cement or building? Try doing a similar exercise with each of your senses, smelling your orange juice for the first time, tasting water for the first time, etc. What is it like, to simply experience without a witness, without an internal judge, or without any kind of worry or planning?

Summation:

Transition: To Find means to allow our senses to serve as open gates to pure awareness, which is both the Kingdom within and the Garden of Paradise without.

To Search means:

1. to prepare to enter into relationship.

2. to be actively open to a transformation of consciousness.

3. to unite and trust inner and outer experience as light along the pathway to our already-present union with God.

4. to be willing to transcend, with the vehicle of simple awareness, the vagaries of words, roles, age, gender and culture in order to see the Beginning Point of our journey.

5. to know we will be successful in our attempt. Indeed, it is inevitable that we shall find because nothing is truly hidden.

6. we cease the endless examination of outward "spiritual" behaviors but rather, focus on an inward change of consciousness.

7. all the pieces of ourselves must come to the Holy Communion table within.

8. we must enter into a process of discernment, ordering our lives around the big and possibly paradigm-changing intuition that arises in us.

9. we must nurture what we are able, both the seeds of wisdom we receive and those we pass on.

10. to look directly into the fire of the cosmos—the movement, transformation, and process that is I AM.

11. to pay attention to the breath-like dance of the two and the one, finally asking what is the movement of those distinctions in Itself?

12. we must stand not for institutions, teachers or books, but for the fire of the cosmos within us.

13. we must leave our comfortable words, concepts and personal mythologies behind so we are open enough to find.

14. to be courageous enough to shake off the dust of traditional or expected actions in favor of entering into a loving relationship with the world.

15. finding the bravery to look into the vast Reality that is the womb from which we've truly sprung.

16. to listen for the still, small voice of a greater unity beneath the cacophony of imposed opinions, rules and institutions.

17. to begin to be willing to explore the intuitive realms that our senses and dualistically conditioned thought processes cannot perceive on their own.

18. to become conscious of the breaking down of opposites, even the great "opposites" of life and death.

Transition Logion: 19. Searching turns to finding when we allow our senses to serve as open gates to pure awareness, which is both the Kingdom within and the Garden of Paradise without, the very process and state of Finding.

The Second Movement: The Logia about Finding

Logion 20

His students said to him,

*"Tell us about this kingdom
of yours in the heavens.
What is it like?"*

Yeshua answered them,

*"Let me compare it to a mustard seed,
the smallest of all the seeds.
When it falls on prepared ground,
it grows into a great tree capable of
sheltering the birds of the sky."*

The First Response:

How can I prepare the ground?
Haunting, is it not,
to rip away the tattered leaves and
dead, twinning roots,
brush aside the ant and slug,
and run fingers into mystery
until fingernails are caked.
But then, after all this effort,
this me-energy,
the bird drops a single seed in a
careless
intuitive
random gesture-
the tiny hint of a tree
that will, in its perfectly
careless
intuitive

random way
open its arms for the same bird's weary body.
Is this not the Kingdom come
at last?

Today in Wisdom's Caravan:

The smallest of seeds are planted every day, and if the soil is prepared, we hope to see that small, curling bit of green emerge. But I sometimes wonder if the preparation is any different from the "careless, intuitive, random" generosity of nature. Perhaps the emphasis in the logion above is less about the prepared soil here than about the ability to accept the grace of the small seed.

All day long, I watch them come to the feeder—nuthatch and chickadee, various thrush and black-eyed towhee. Seeds fly all over, some consumed, some given to the wind. In the breezy rain today, some of that seed is germinating beneath the feeder, and I suspect, somewhere in my moss-covered wood or out in the back pasture, seed has been dropped and is even now taking root. The mustard is an invasive plant; it generally is not content to create a single tree standing alone in a carefully prepared agricultural field—it spreads rapidly and is more difficult to root out than our Scotch Broom here in the Pacific Northwest. It takes over and becomes the dominant energy in the field.

So how does a small seed of consciousness bloom in ourselves? We might never have realized how the ground was prepared to receive that awakening, but one thing is assured: we will be changed, the mustard seed disturbing the neat rows and carefully polite lines of cultural conditioning until we can throw open our arms to all, even the stranger brought to us on the wing.

Ameyn.

The Eastern Parallels:

"External nature is only internal nature writ large.
You have to grow from the inside out. None can teach you,
none can make you spiritual. There is no other teacher but
your own soul. It is *feeling* that is the life, the strength, the
vitality, without which no amount of intellectual activity can
reach God."

--Vivekananda

Going Deeper:

As you consider your faith today, can you pinpoint ways you
prepare the ground for interior growth? Or does your faith
seem, instead, to have existed in a random way, sprung up from
little seeds gifted to you by life? Did your spiritual practices
start this seedling of faith or did they come out of a learned kind
of faith? This is often a grace-filled question to ask.

Summation:

**To Find is to allow ourselves to be gifted with the smallest
seeds of the great Tree of Life.**

Logion 21

Miriam said,
"Then tell us, Master,
what are your students like?
How would you describe them"?

He answered,
"They are like small children
living in a field not their own.
When the landlords return and demand,
'Give us back our field!'
the children return it by
simply stripping themselves
and standing naked before them.

So then, I must also tell you this:
If a householder knows for sure that
thieves are coming to steal his goods,
he will keep careful watch before they
get there to prevent them from tunneling
in and taking his possessions.
You, too, from your beginnings,
must keep a watchful eye on the cosmos,
binding great power to yourselves
so that thieves cannot find a way
to get to you.
Pay attention then.
Any outside help you look for,
they will try to seize first.
May there be someone among you
who truly understands this.
So listen carefully,
if you have an ear for this!
When the fruit was ripe,
ready to burst

the harvester came quickly,
sickle in hand,
and took it."

The First Response:

I might have bowed when I was young,
naked before the owner of the field—willing to take
anyone older and more powerful at face value,
human or God
for that matter.

As I aged, I certainly learned to shore up my walls,
defend my sense of house, home,
self--
willing to be the warrior, the owner,
the one who was perpetually ready to repulse
human thieves or God
for that matter.

But now,
I am somewhere in between.
Perhaps as I ripen, I will neither bow to others nor
think I can plan for every contingency.
Maybe in ripening,
I am finding my way
at last
to
Thy Will Be Done,
playing with humans and God
where there are no walls,
finding only sweet flesh
in
the things
that
may or

may not
matter.

Today in Wisdom's Caravan:

This has always been one of the trickier logion in this
particular cycle of finding. Today, I see it one way, and
tomorrow, I may see it in a wholly different way. Actually, I like
that discontinuity within myself; it probably means this logion
really has to be "lived into" in each season of our lives. Often,
when three short metaphors are stacked like this, a reader can
a) look for the syncretism between them, the way they are
saying the same thing in different ways; or b) see the
progression within them, the way each state leads historically
from a simple to a more "ripened" way of understanding; or c)
something that is a little of both.

I tend to look at this logion as "c"--the metaphors all talk
about how to be in relationship with God and all are critical to
our relationship with our world develops as well. In one sense,
when we begin the spiritual path, we have to stand naked like
the children at play in the field, but there is no discernment in
that movement. It is purely open, trusting, and we have no
ground to defend. But it is also like the fool's card in the tarot.
We don't own the field, we have no opinions, no experiences.
This is the springtime flower on the fruit tree. We aren't in
relationship particularly; we are ordered and we acquiesce
because we haven't done the work yet of discernment.

Next, we must understand what we stand for and find
the treasure we think is God. It is an idea worth defending
within the four solid walls of our hearts. This is the stage of
dualism, me defining what I do and do not **believe**. We are
ripening, seeing the world in black and white, in and out, no
longer a child but also separate, lonely, and defensive in our
minds and hearts. We bind great power to ourselves—creeds,
dogmas, beliefs, the shadow of the tribe that creates walls and

where thieves may tunnel in. We are like a hard fruit, no sugar within yet, stiff, unyielding and thinking we have found home.

Finally, we ripen and in that ripening, must wholly yield to God, no longer innocent and naked, no longer defensive and dualistic. We are the fruit full of sugar and hanging heavy in space, playing in the field, no walls, ready to nurture others by giving up our very lives, if necessary, when God comes for the harvest. We come again to the theme of Yes, dying to ourselves, both the child and the householder and even finally, to our precious sense of self.

Ameyn.

The Eastern Parallels:

"It is better to live your own destiny imperfectly than to live an imitation of somebody else's life with perfection."

— The Bhagavad Gita

"A gift is pure when it is given from the heart to the right person at the right time and at the right place, and when we expect nothing in return."

— The Bhagavad Gita

"The peace of God is with them whose mind and soul are in harmony, who are free from desire and wrath, who know their own soul."

— The Bhagavad Gita

Going Deeper:

Place one hand on your heart and one on your belly. Breathe into that lower hand, feeling it moving as your upper hand stays still. Let the peace of that paradox enter into you...movement and stillness touched beneath the palms of your hands, unified in the ripe totality of yourself.

Summation:

To Find means to be willing to see the ripening happening within ourselves that cannot be hurried or pressed into a human sense of completion.

Logion 22

Yeshua noticed infants nursing and said
to his students,

"These little ones taking milk are
like those on the way to the kingdom."

So they asked him,
"If we too are 'little ones'
are we on our way into the kingdom?"

Yeshua replied,
"When you are able
to make two become one,
the inside like the outside,
and the outside like the inside,
the higher like the lower,
so that a man is no longer male,
and a woman, female
but male and female become a single whole;
when you are able to fashion
an eye to replace an eye
and form a hand in place of a hand,
or a foot for a foot
making one image supercede another—
then you will enter in."

The First Response:

Are we not, all of us,
the answer to every paradox?
From two came one,
sexual union
then

a fetus
now female, now male—
mixing and trading genders in the darkness.
Did we not sense the oneness in that womb,
and even when we became two,
our tiny lungs gasping in our first taste of separation,
(we cried, remember?)
we, you, me, I
returned again to a oneness to suckle,
both fed and satisfied at once?

In every creative act we dance,
first one, then two, then one again;
seer and seen,
leaping
from that union of eye with form
only to swirl together
in the unity of consciousness,
the place where
we dip
and put brush to canvas.

No great effort to see and then
form foot from foot
or hand from hand--
it is as easy as
just catching that playful blink
that separates the
elements
of
every
paradox.

Today in Wisdom's Caravan:

The disciples demonstrate anew that their dualistic and literal world does not give way readily to Yeshua, who is able to see ultimate reality and relative reality in a single glance. He once again tries to expand their mind by showing and not telling, by using metaphor to take them from their present state of seeing the world to a wider vision.

I have a great trust of paradox and process. When I see Yeshua's words, lining up opposites, then transcending them, I find myself smiling. He sounds like a riddle master, but truly, he is speaking an absolute Truth to his students. If we consider our mind, our consciousness, singular behind closed eyes, then open our eyes to see a writing pen, we can feel the interplay between mind and an object observed. That is the first shift—one to two. Then, we can feel how, when we shut our eyes, we can hold the image of the pen within. But mind and pen here have become one, actually became one the moment our eye fell on it in "outer" reality. We just slowed the process down, gave it space to be observed. Reality is nothing other than mind, no matter if we separate ourselves from it or watch the shift from two to one to two, always shimmering.

I believe Yeshua is also playing with the creative aspect of mind—once we have seen and experienced one "foot", we can expand on that theme, making little feet, big feet, purple feet, etc. And yes, we can see each foot as if for the first time, without even naming it, wholly caught up and of one mind with the foot. We may also recall foot memories, foot dreams, anticipate clothing our foot with the latest fashion. Foot is nothing other than mind, malleable and contingent upon the attention or creative energy we bring to it.

So in the spirit of open attentiveness and in allowing ourselves to be held in like regard, we are like children. But we have will—and discernment—that a baby does not. Both those elements can be tools or impediments on the spiritual journey, and Yeshua is already pointing to sticking places like gender,

age, what is in and out, what is higher and lower where our attention must become more fluid and generous and whole.
   Ameyn.

The Eastern Parallels:

"The first veil to vanish is ignorance; and
when that is gone, unskillful behavior goes;
next desire ceases,
selfishness ends, and
all misery disappears."

--Yogananda

"Just as, my dear, by one clod of clay all that is made of clay is known, the modification being only a name, arising from speech, while the truth is that all is clay; Just as, my dear, by one nugget of gold all that is made of gold is known, the modification being only a name, arising from speech, while the truth is that all is gold..."

--Chandogya Upanishad 6:1:2-6

Aum.
Asato ma sad-gamaya;
tamaso ma jyotir-gamaya;
mrtyor-ma amrutam gamaya.
Aum. Shanti, shanti, shanti.

Translation:
Aum. Lead me from unreal to real;
lead me from darkness to light;
lead me from death to immortality.
Aum... peace, peace, peace.

--Brihadaranyaka Upanishad

Going Deeper:

Sit in a quiet place today, watching your breath. At first, you will feel light and expansive with the in-breath, and then heavier and grounded with the out-breath. Without forcing, just keep watching the breath. Notice how it slows, quiets, and may almost seem to stop. In that place of stillness, in is out, out is in, and breath and you are one. Now gently begin to encourage your breath to deepen. What happens to your sense of body, breath, mind? How quickly does movement want to follow the breath?

Summation:

To Find means to use the gifts of attention, creativity, and will with a child's sense of belonging and place.

Logion 23

Yeshua says

*"I choose you,
one from a thousand,
two from ten-thousand,
and you will stand to your own feet
having become single
and whole."*

The First Response:

I notice what is missing—
when a number is given,
hinting at
special-ness,
choseness,
I automatically
understand it in terms of human beings.
One in ten-thousand...
but really, ten-thousand
whatsits?

I miss how we all stand up out of
clay and rock,
wave and sky,
fir, birdseed,
wing,
four-legged ones,
scales and forked tongues,
and bi-hooves
ice and stars
dust and waterfalls.

But then, maybe,
those entities don't need to recognize themselves
as already single and whole,
as
endlessly and effortlessly
standing.

Today in Wisdom's Caravan:

In Buddhism and Hinduism, sometimes our lucky human birth is described like this: imagine a single turtle, swimming around in a world with no land masses. Now imagine as well a single, floating life preserver bobbing on those endless waves. The human birth and life is as rare as the times that one turtle surfaces and sticks his head through the circle when he takes a breath. That is the very definition of why our lives are precious, why spiritual practice and waking up should feel like running toward water when your very hair is on fire.

The trick, it seems to me, is to not forget that really, everything around us is just as unique, life-filled and chosen. When we look up into the sky, and really get a sense of how small our little world is, how small our little country, how incredibly small our little selves are, we better understand what Yeshua means when he asks us to stand. Because we are the conscious ones, the ones created by God to use all our senses so that God might know her/his/its very nature. Not because we can name, not because we can create theologies or ideas or dogmas or religions, but because we can use our senses with consciousness and a startling awareness of choice in our reactions to sense impressions and thoughts.

There is also a deep sense of the *chosen beloved* here, and I must remind myself not to miss that. Otherwise, my paragraphs above begin to sound a little dry and abstract. We can only stand in all of this already-standing miracle of life and planet and space if we do so with the touchstone of compassion that sees how much we are held by this web. Standing does not imply individual warrior strength alone (although that is part of it); it also requires our full awareness of our relationship with all we can sense and with what we cannot. If we take away the love, the heart-response, the cherishing and cherished, we will only be poverty stricken within.

Ameyn.

The Eastern Parallels:

"Ask yourself how many of the billions of the inhabitants of the planet have any idea of how rare it is to have been born as a human being. How many of those who understand the rarity of human birth ever think of even using that chance to practice the Dharma? How many of those who think of practice actually do practice? How many of those who start really continue? How many of those who practice continue and attain ultimate realization? Indeed those who attain ultimate realization compared to those who do not are as few as the stars you can see at daybreak. As long as you fail to recognize the true value of human existence, you will just fritter your life away in futile activity and distraction. When life comes all too soon to its inevitable end, you will not have achieved anything worthwhile at all. But once you really see the unique opportunity that human life can bring, you will definitely direct all your energy into reaping its true worth."

--Dilgo Khyentse Rinpoche

"We are not having this precious human birth in the world just to fill the stomach, produce offspring, and die; we should be ready to live and leave with the fulfillment of a deeply realized life."

--Swami Iraianban in
Preaching Vedanta

116

"Therefore the doubts which have arisen in your heart out of ignorance should be slashed by the weapon of knowledge. Armed with yoga, O Bharata, stand and fight for the living Dharma."

--The Bhagavad-Gita

Going Deeper:

I remember being told to never ask "why" in graduate school as a method of analysis or the basis to forming a hypothesis. But when I look at my life, "why" is the great question, the base question, the ground question. Consider today how the question "why?" informs your spirituality.

Summation:

To Find means to fully recognize your unique sovereignty and utter interdependency with all of life.

Logion 24

His students said to him,

"Take us to the place where you are
since we are required to seek after it."

He answered them,

"Whoever has an ear for this
should listen carefully!
Light shines out from the center
of a being of light
and illuminates the whole cosmos.
Whoever fails to become light
is a source of darkness."

The First Response:

We are not created to be solid,
nor rooted in place like the massive cedar
standing sentinel in my front yard.
The statue fascinates
because it is almost alive,
because sometimes
we see the light moving
in carved pupils.
But we are called to the wave's way,
to be tidal and restless
and hold mystery under our froth.
We wet the stone,
lick the sand,
carry the whale and the krill with equal ease.
Diving into our own liquid darkness,
see how we shine
even in the dim starlight?

Today in Wisdom's Caravan:

Truly, it's harder to be less clear than this message—we are called to be as Yeshua is himself, called into the ranks of those who give light from their very being. It's a hard thing to hear though. We have a propensity to prefer worship to transformation, and yet here, in a reply that starts with "listen up!" we are told that straight-up truth.

It is wildly difficult to stand up and be as our "hero" *is*, rather than stand back and applaud at the right places or have the freedom to turn away when that suits us. To be the actual light-bringer, to step into the role that Yeshua has mimed out for us, is terrifying. It asks for all of us, not just the bits that want to be comforted, entertained, or intellectually satisfied. Were it not for the fact that we are already deeply like him in our cores, in our very natures as God's creations, we might not feel at all up to the "finding" that searching demands.

In a sense, we are called to acknowledge our birthrights, to hold back the dark and to go bravely into the search *because* we have this model of Yeshua as our teacher. Yet even here, we are being told not to cling to him, that he cannot "make" us other than we already are, and that salvation, if we wish to call it that, is accomplished by standing up into the fullness of God within and as *ourselves*. If we are being nurtured, partnered, instructed and treasured by our teacher, then it is so that those seeds will bloom in us and *as us*, and allow us to pass such light onward.

Ameyn.

The Eastern Parallels:

"When I Asked God for Strength
He Gave Me Difficult Situations to Face

When I Asked God for Brain & Brawn
He Gave Me Puzzles in Life to Solve

119

When I Asked God for Happiness
He Showed Me Some Unhappy People

When I Asked God for Wealth
He Showed Me How to Work Hard

When I Asked God for Favors
He Showed Me Opportunities to Work Hard

When I Asked God for Peace
He Showed Me How to Help Others

God Gave Me Nothing I Wanted
He Gave Me Everything I Needed."

— Swami Vivekananda

"You have to grow from the inside out. None can teach you, none can make you spiritual. There is no other teacher but your own soul."

— Swami Vivekananda

Going Deeper:

Sit gently with the idea that your highest image of the divine, in whatever form is true to you, is actually mirroring the light that you yourself have within. Gently take up your journal and write what comes to mind. Does this create a sense of fear in you? Sadness? Joy and animation? Where do these states rest in your body? What was their origin?

Summation:

To Find is to accept with full awareness that we are not called to worship, but rather, to stand and shine forth who we were all created to be.

Logion 25

Yeshua says,

*"Love your brother and your sister
as your very own being.
Protect them as you would
the pupil of your eye."*

The First Response:

Permeable,
this scrubbed and perfumed
second lung,
this skin available in so
many shades and hues.
How we armor it all,
with clothes and make-up
with jewelry and shoes
with shampoo and soap and deodorant.

Permeable, too, this breathing pupil
this black dot that expands and contracts to
help
discern
light
in
around
with and
through
form.

Light!

And in us all, it is a pregnant darkness, no matter
what finery rims it round.

Today in Wisdom's Caravan:

I enjoyed slowing down with this logion today, and using it for Lectio Divina and poetry. Its very simplicity hides the depths Yeshua is showing us in his usual subtle way. At first glance, the message of loving thy neighbor as thyself hits us because that is how we have trained our "ear to hear". And we may be tempted to stop there.

But what *is* a brother or a sister? Mere blood relation? Mere associative names within the four walls of a community, like when we call a church member a "brother" or "sister"? I've been enjoying listening to folks getting back their DNA assessments that show their genetic family trees. Many claim to have Neanderthal markers in them! How funny, amazing and profound such a realization is.

And this pupil in our eye is all about discernment; the gateway that allows just the right amount of light into the complex system that distinguishes form, texture, details. I use the word "discern" with all seriousness because that is the secondary message here—*how much "light" can you discern if you lose your brothers and sisters, if you lose the community that is all humankind*? Like any part of this searching process, you could limit this teaching to relatives and real physical eyeballs. But the message is so much bigger than the personal.

Ameyn.

The Eastern Parallels:

"They alone live, who live for others."

— Swami Vivekananda

"All love is expansion, all selfishness is contraction. Love is therefore the only law of life. He who loves lives, he who is selfish is dying. Therefore love for love's sake, because it is the only law of life, just as you breathe to live."

— Swami Vivekananda

"Where can we go to find God if we cannot see Him in our own hearts and in every living being?"

— Swami Vivekananda

Going Deeper:

Close your eyes and breathe deeply for a moment, centering yourself. And then, consider a close friend, feeling the compassion you hold for them. Then try to picture their friends, their friend's friends, taking the levels of association out and out as far as you can imagine. Who is brother, who is sister, really?

Summation:

To Find means to preserve and cherish the larger community that helps us discern light.

Logion 26

Yeshua says,

"You detect a speck
in your brother's eye,
but fail to perceive the beam
sticking out of your own.
Remove the timber from your eye,
and you will see clearly enough
to extract the speck lodged
in the eye of your brother."

The First Response:

Hello, shadow.
I've set out a bright light,
here, where I can switch it on easily,
so you don't have to fade into that weird grayness
of the florescent overheads.
Funny how businesses and hospitals
try not to cast any shadows.
I know you are resting behind me right now,
breathing as I breathe,
and if I just turn a bit
I can see you.
I've poured us a cup of stiff, black coffee and we can watch
how the trees lattice the lawn
and the hawk shadow
threads through lines of light.

Today in Wisdom's Caravan:

Many of us will recognize Yeshua's words from Matthew
7:4-5 and Luke 6:41-42, but there is a critical difference here,

too, because the words of the Gospel of Thomas command us to remove the timber or plank—an injunction that is merely implicit in the Synoptic Gospels.   There is no gentleness here, either. Yeshua says, "remove it." And why? So then you can help your brother or sister with their own blocked vision.

There is always a strong current of relationship running through the words of this wisdom teacher, and with that relationship, a cooperative sense of awakening not for our own sake, but for the sake of those around us as well. Buddhist practitioners may well recognize a bodhisattva spirit that plays through these ancient words.

Of course, this logion is also a continuation of protecting the pupil of your eye, a subject we explored in logion 25. This link brings us back to the idea of discernment, an important part of the spiritual search. Where we are blind, where the shadow is at play, we lose a whole chunk of reality and with it, the ability to make sound choices on our spiritual journeys.

Finally, the eye is only one of the "evergreen trees", the routes through which our limited understanding of tangible reality can flow. Yeshua is asking us to seek that which informs the eye, the part that will allow us to "see" even if we were born physically blind. So again, this is an invitation into his deeper reality.

Ameyn.

The Eastern Parallels:

"We are responsible for what we are, and whatever we wish ourselves to be, we have the power to make ourselves. If what we are now has been the result of our own past actions, it certainly follows that whatever we wish to be in the future can be produced by our present actions; so we have to know how to act."

— Swami Vivekananda

Going Deeper:

Thomas Merton pointed out on many occasions that the distractions of our culture are the 'beam in our eye'. What distractions keep you from your spiritual path? Name them, bring them into the light, where you can discern their purpose and meaning for yourself.

Summation:

To Find means to open to all of ourselves, including our shadows, so that we might be of discerning service to others.

Logion 27

Yeshua says,

"If you do not fast from the cosmos,
you will never grasp Reality.
If you cannot find rest
on the day of rest
you will never feast
your eyes on God."

The First Response:

Traffic lights, rain reflections,
wind breaks a tree branch off,
shopping list, spilled cereal,
deadline, calendar,
past conversation, present sunlight on the teaching whiteboard
squeaking tennis shoes, coffee scents,
Hannibal on television,
son yells upstairs, another point scored
in another reality of dragons and swords.
The buffet of life can fill pages—I know,
I write the best bits down, sweat them out in prose and
short, quick lines
and
watch them fade as I sink a little below them,
my knees folded, my hands in my lap
breath catching a little as
this memory,
that plan
those emotions
dive down to entice me,
like cookies and chocolate.

One lonely bird at the feeder today,

128

black head, gray body--
nothing to do just now
but watch the feathered face of God
feasting.

What was I doing that was so important?
Already, I am rested, filled and
it is the day
called Sabbath,
Wednesday,
every day.

Today in Wisdom's Caravan:

Feasts and fasts, poverty and wealth, cosmos and reality, the face of God and unseen ground of being, rest and the day set aside for it, there is much going on here in these simple lines. The dualistic language almost rocks us, and for once seems perfectly simple. In all likelihood, we would just turn the page, thinking we know what is being communicated, that the message is literally given to us in this logion--set aside time to rest and know God—Next!

But we are in the uncertain territory of "finding" in this section of the Gospel of Thomas—we *are* hunger, we *are* poverty, we *are* all about rules and observances (a day of rest, a fast and the goal of seeing the face of God). Notice that Yeshua isn't telling us how to do any of the explicit activities above. As our teacher, he is sending us a subtle challenge—how can you work rest into your daily life? How can you fast from the entire cosmos? What is the face of God to you?

In a sense, he is gently poking us to move beyond these dualities (about which many self-help books are written) into a life that is non-dual. The best way to fast from the cosmos is to find your life filled with spaciousness and openness, the best day for rest is not different from a day of mindful activity, and

129

the face of God is everywhere always available. We stop lying to ourselves about our prayer life, our "contemplative life", our "rest" and "fasting" being anything other than each moment of our lives, nothing special, yet everything amazing.

Ameyn.

The Eastern Parallels:

"The power of God is with you at all times, through the activities of mind, senses, breathing, and emotions, and is constantly doing all the work using you as a mere instrument."

- The Bhagavad-Gita

"Perform all thy actions with mind concentrated on the Divine, renouncing attachment and looking upon success and failure with an equal eye. Spirituality implies equanimity."

- The Bhagavad-Gita

"You have the right to work, but never to the fruit of work. You should never engage in action for the sake of reward, nor should you long for inaction. Perform work in this world, Arjuna, as a man established within himself - without selfish attachments, and alike in success and defeat."

-The Bhagavad-Gita

Going Deeper:

Chogyam Trungpa once wrote an important book about what he called "spiritual materialism"—the tendency to make of our living in spirit something "special" or "acquired" or "objectified". As you think of your life, do you create artificial divides between life and "spirit"? How might you soften these lines?

Summation:

To Find means to begin to see through the division between the sacred and the profane, between the acts and concepts of religion and the life of the spirit.

Logion 28

Yeshua says,

*"I stood to my feet
in the midst of the cosmos,
appearing outwardly in flesh.
I discovered that all were drunk
and none were thirsty,
and my soul ached for
the children of humanity.
For their hearts are blind
and they cannot see from within.
They have come into the cosmos empty,
and they are leaving it empty.
At the moment, you are inebriated,
but free from the effects of wine,
you too may turn and stand."*

The First Response:

Until you believe
with each inhale
you share in the very rise and falls of stars,
emptiness
will fill you instead.
Until you see that
standing,
you connect heaven and earth,
you are blind
to even the presence of light.
Until you hear that pure note
ringing through everything,
everyone,
you crouch alone,

hands covering your head,
and this fecund mud
of your mind
will never really appreciate
the flesh that wants to bloom.

Today in Wisdom's Caravan:

Yeshua is speaking here of what Buddhists would call ignorance—an inability to move beyond the dualist mind and see the spaciousness and interconnected web of reality that is as close to us as our own breath and skin. Just like alcohol can put us at a short distance from our fears, our real selves, and relationships, so, too, does the inability to stand up and hold both the relative and ultimate forms of reality bind us to inner poverty.

My heart hitched a bit today because I could feel the Yeshua's frustration and sadness that people around him were stuck in their little, personal lives. Even that pain, though, is what fueled this wisdom teacher to keep rephrasing his words in parables, to stay on the road and to keep trying to reach people. In other words, his pain in the inability of people to awaken to the gifts of God surely became part of what kept him teaching with greater *creativity* instead of pushing him to shut up and give up.

What Yeshua is trying to offer his disciples is nothing short of what he himself experiences and lives in, and through these words, the offer is also extended to us. Or rather, he is trying to show us we already live in this world, and all we have to do is stand up and realize it. It's like the end of a perfect sermon; when we stand, we integrate all that has come before, making it part of us, so it informs what comes after. And that moment of standing is always the work of the present moment, wide-eyed and breathing deeply.

Ameyn.

The Eastern Parallels:

"God is in all men, but all men are not in God; that is why we suffer."

--Ramakrishna

"Bondage is of the mind; freedom too is of the mind. If you say 'I am a free soul. I am a son of God who can bind me?' free you shall be."

--Ramakrishna

Going Deeper:

Today, as you go about your work, try to use your senses to take small sips of the larger cycles of life, of beauty, of your relationship with others. Don't over-think anything, just notice. At the end of the day, assess how you feel. This is one part of what Yeshua means when he asks us to "stand."

Summation:

To Find means to be willing to throw off our inebriation and stand up into both relative and ultimate reality.

Logion 29

Yeshua says,

"If flesh came into existence
for the sake of spirit,
it is a wonder.
But if spirit exists for the sake of flesh,
it is a wonder of wonders.
I am truly astonished
at how such richness
came to dwell in such poverty."

The First Response:

Season of Lent,
Gregorian chant resonating, as always, when I write,
skies gray, same with my shirt,
deep forest views so
no flowers,
just birds practicing meditative hops
beneath their half-stocked feeder.
Pile of tenacious vines heaped by one fence,
St. Francis statue finally turning a little mossy
standing, as he does, in a pile of found shells.
Munching hot wasabi peas,
now and again glancing at the cover of a book—
something about Icon writing.

I don't think I need to open it just yet.

Today in Wisdom's Caravan:

Such a small turn of mind—not a spiritual being having a human experience, but a human opening to the vast richness of the world around us that is spirit-filled. And in that turning, we finally touch with humbleness and delight, the same play of spirit within. It's like being lifted by a wave, like finally understanding the taste of really excellent dark chocolate, or feeling like Mozart did when he said the universe had left music for him to find.

I find nothing in this that calls us to poverty, or subservient bowing, but I do recognize humor, a child-like interest, and the textures of relationship in Yeshua's gentle turn-around about how many of us understand indwelling spirit. Any lack of wealth is simply bound to an inability to open the senses and catch the icons all around us, all the time, and by that seeing, acknowledge the wealth that is in ourselves and everything else. It is a unified spirit, a relational spirit, whistling up attention and intention.

Flesh is not something secondary; it is the vehicle through which we awaken. Spirit serves us by enlivening us, calling us out to be bigger, more sensitive, more engaged by the millions of daily recognitions of spirit calling us to spirit. Rather than the model of "in" to the heart, then "up to heaven" and "out of the cyclic nature of existence (the daily grind?)", Yeshua calls us out into the world to recognize our own heart and then understand that there never was an up or down, an in or an out. Or even *real* poverty and wealth.

"God became man so man could become God" as early theologians in the Christian tradition said.

Ameyn.

The Eastern Parallels:

"You see many stars in the sky at night, but not when the sun rises. Can you therefore say that there are no stars in the heavens during the day? Because you cannot find God in the days of your ignorance, say not that there is no God."

— Ramakrishna

"When divine vision is attained, all appear equal; and there remains no distinction of good and bad, or of high and low."

— Ramakrishna

Going Deeper:

First, bow deeply and think to yourself, I exist for the spirit. Now, bow deeply and think to yourself, the spirit exists for me. Stand and feel the reality of both states—can you feel how you are in relationship, not one idea of yourself or the divine above the other?

Summation:

To Find means to be willing to acknowledge with each breath we do not exist for spirit—spirit also exists for us.

Logion 30

Yeshua says,

"Where there are
three divinities,
God is present.
Where one or two exist,
I am there."

The First Response:

Three works for me—
heaven and earth and human linking them,
Godhead and prophet and human conflating them,
Mother and Maiden and Crone,
triskele—
I could go on, but this is a dance you know.
Still,
it is in our nature to number and name
from states of mind to stars in the galaxy;
maybe that's not all bad—
it means that we are present
and
engaged
and hopefully
eventually
w(holy) relational.

Today in Wisdom's Caravan:

I see in this Logion a call to conscious awareness of the relationships we are surrounded with always, as well as a cautionary note. When we attend, first there is the pure seeing and relating, then the naming and numbering comes, and from that the outer verbalization of reality. We *think* we know it. Perhaps as part of finding, this categorization is initially useful and even necessary because it illustrates how our minds work.

Yet, I love how Yeshua gently moves the mind to understand that, if we can sense "three divinities" then we can also sense the great I AM that unites them. Glimpse it just once, and each time we are face to face with another, we will sense it. It is a call to use the intuitive sense, to engage our sensitivity to Presence. He is using mind to move beyond the analytic function of mind, a classic wisdom teacher technique.

So reading this becomes startling when we stop counting and trying to name the three divinities because they are not truly separate—the three are one, as in the later formulation of the Christian trinity. And the number three can be conflated to a hundred, a million, countless souls. "Together" the three divinities *are* God.

When two gather, separated, that way of seeing still exists. Yeshua's I AM is there as well, but notice they do not then become aware of God because they are not touching the divinity that they are. And they merely *exist*—bound by culture, bias, time. I wonder if Yeshua felt a passing sadness here— "They exist and I am there": the "I" that we can eventually learn to realize is both the egoic personal AND the transpersonal.

Ameyn.

The Eastern Parallels:

"There is One who is the eternal Reality among non-eternal objects, the one [truly] conscious Entity among conscious objects, and who, though non-dual, fulfills the desires of many.

139

Eternal peace belongs to the wise, who perceive Him within themselves—not to others."

--Katha Upanishad

"To the seer, all things have verily become the Self: what delusion, what sorrow, can there be for him who beholds that oneness?"

--Isha Upanishad

Going Deeper:

As you go about your day today, try to see God within each person. That measure of respect and awe and discomfort and forgetfulness you will encounter will remind you of the relational quality of our lives together. It is not a practice of guilt! Do not chastise yourself when you cannot maintain that kind of awareness, but rather, make it a practice of musical notes, learning to hear melody in a way that is not about words, analysis nor self blame.

Summation:

To Find means to be willing to claim the unifying divinity that under girds the many and varied individuals.

Logion 31

Yeshua says,

"No prophet is
welcomed home.
No healer cures acquaintances."

The First Response:

Can you really see me?
is the silent cry of humanity—
it shadows the self-help section of the library,
rides in the new car,
the latest fashion,
the makeup counter
and
the gym.
Insidious
it plays as well in
alleyways where drugs go hand to shaking hand
in the curved reflection of the whiskey bottle.
Friends may be the worst mirrors of all
if each time you meet,
you think
only of the changeless nature
of masks.
What we name we think we know.
And we will always only see
what we think.

Today in Wisdom's Caravan:

This logion is really saying a similar thing as the previous one; in our "thinking" that we know someone, we don't allow for change, growth nor "see the message" of divinity that is the voice of prophet and healer. By boxing the other in with our conceptual understanding of him or her, we also cut ourselves off from the message and health that they could hand us without effort and usually with no sense of reward.

What Yeshua is teaching is very pragmatic on one level; I'm sure we've all had the experience of people not able to see us as we really are because they remember a past version of us. Or perhaps you've found, in the round of daily interactions, others have created a "model" or "mask" that represents you so they can place you in a psychological landscape as a dependable and unchanging *object*.

But a prophet and a healer cannot be objectified—they both bring messages that must shine through their entire selves, indeed, must shine out from the center of their hearts. If they are not seen without bias, the ear will always be stuffed closed, the eye clouded with the seer's own agendas. In short, we must be able to see the divinity within them, something that is very hard to do if we think we already know them in all their complexity and depth.

Ameyn.

The Eastern Parallels:

"You cannot see That which is the Seer of seeing; you cannot hear That which is the Hearer of hearing; you cannot think of That which is the Thinker of thought; you cannot know That which is the Knower of knowledge. This is your Self, that is within all; everything else but This is perishable."

--Brihadaranyaka Upanishad

"Thinking of You (Krishna) as my friend, I have rashly addressed You "O Kṛṣṇa," "O Yādava," "O my friend," not knowing Your glories. Please forgive whatever I may have done in madness or in love. I have dishonored You many times, jesting as we relaxed, lay on the same bed, or sat or ate together, sometimes alone and sometimes in front of many friends. O infallible one, please excuse me for all those offenses."

-The Bhagavad-Gita

Going Deeper:

Today, as you go about your day, try to meet friends and acquaintances as if you had never talked with them before. See something new, get curious about their lives, their wisdom. This small act of trying to really see them again will not just bless them, it will bless you as well.

Summation:

To Find means to truly see the divinity in all those around you, transcending your own tendency to mask and objectify them.

Logion 32

Yeshua says,

"A city built and fortified
on a mountain top cannot fall,
but neither can it be hidden."

The First Response:

The tiny frog sings out in the falling rain,
uneven,
listening between each note,
the cold spring drops tracing rivulets across
his tan and brown hide.
He tucks in close, tender belly against the tree,
but still it rises in him,
boiling up through his small spine,
expanding his throat
erupting in one clear call of life,
then hunkering again into the flex of his tiny toes
as the shadow of the raccoon slinks by.
The frog holds his breath a moment,
knows the truth,
viscerally--
speak your creative truth,
but hold tight to the roots of your tree.

Today in Wisdom's Caravan:

This logion brings the inevitable good news/bad news of
finding--when you begin to see you will of course observe the
truth like a city on a hill, seemingly impregnable but also
undeniably clear. It holds for you a kind of tension—what is

visible from without can also be hidden within, its full truth behind walls and seemingly barricaded from us. The hope that springs within is that someday, *you will see the city from the inside*, transparent to all but also settled deeply into the bones of the mountain where you might both reign and rest. Seeing that possibility, of entering to the very foundations of yourself and finding there the graceful and unhidden quality of the inner city on the hill, becomes the beacon of hope for us.

It also calls us to consider that we must open those city gates, coming and going as the breath does, bringing life within those grounded walls, and breathing out to a greater world. Searching for the faith of Yeshua is not about defensive holding within old traditions or old paradigms but rather the visible and courageous opening outward as well. That is the mountain of faith on which the city is built, not simply a hunkering and closed system which would not survive. Notice how Yeshua expands on this idea in the next logion.

Ameyn.

The Eastern Parallels:

"He who is rooted in oneness
realizes that I am
in every being; wherever
he goes, he remains in me."

--The Bhagavad-Gita

"The more we come out and do good to others, the more our hearts will be purified, and God will be in them."

--Swami Vivekananda

Going Deeper:

As you take your meditation seat today, rock gently back and forth and side to side. Feel the earth supporting you and then, as you settle into stillness, breathe mindfully. Consider the flowing and ephemeral nature of this basis of life, so unhindered and pulsing with activity and yet how it is held in the stable bones of your pelvis and spine and ribs. Picture the city on the hill, its gates thrown open, so that the breath-traveler can enter and leave consciously.

Summation:

To Find means to move beyond observing life into the pulsing energy of participation.

Logion 33

Yeshua says,

"What you hear with one ear
listen to with both,
and then proclaim
from the rooftops.
For no one lights a lamp
and then hides it away.
It is placed on a lamp-stand instead
where those who pass by
may see by its light."

The First Response:

We do not search for just ourselves.
In what dim glow we find,
one hand reaches for another,
instinctively
creatively—

plant a seed and does it not
lean in toward the sun?
Plant a thousand sunflower seeds,
and a riot of brilliant yellow
will track that blazing kin across the sky,
feet planted in the earth,
but oh,
each head full of a thousand seeds,
awaiting their own
rich
soil.

Today in Wisdom's Caravan:

We can learn to listen with both the ear of the mind and the ear of the heart. In tandem, we "hear" the whole symphony of meaning in the world around us. Much of that learning is simply attention, but it also utilizes compassion, engaged interest, and relational presence.

It's important to notice that Yeshua again reflects this idea that our spiritual awakening is not in service to our personal egos, but rather, we must help shine this light for others. Further along in this Gospel, he'll try to show us how we might do such a thing—shine and shout from rooftops without a personal ego-attachment to that act of sharing. He is not necessarily talking about teaching here; rather, how do we manifest the realizations we have made in daily living?

Ameyn.

The Eastern Parallels:

"This is That -- thus they realize the ineffable joy supreme. How can "This" be known? Does he give light or does he reflect light?"

--Katha Upanishad

"Words and mind go to him, but reach him not and return. But he who knows the joy of Brahman, fears no more."

--Taittiriya Upanishad

Going Deeper:

How do you share with others your insights about how reality functions? Do you use a "formal" creative voice (poetry, writing, painting, music, etc) or do you prefer the "informal" creative voice whether it is the meal well planned, the smile and hello for the check-out clerk, the listening ear for a friend? Is your life a mix of these two movements? In what way does this creative voice pass on the message of Yeshua?

Summation:

To Find means to be willing to share our discoveries, helping to create the bonds of relationship.

Logion 34

Yeshua says,

**"If the blind are leading the blind
they will topple together
into a pit."**

The First Response:

In darkness, better to take that sliding step,
let your toes grow eyes,
heels
learning how to sink and anchor;
don't worry how long it takes—
what is time in this place where you
cannot see the clock?
What sounds and sensations now
tickle you
in ways once easily ignored,
so driven were you,
your right arm hitched up behind you,
your shoulder pushed to your ear
by the blind rush along
the lip
of
the
abyss?

Choose to not be pushed or led.

Your path will smooth out in time,
a dancing beneath a wide and brilliant sky.

Today in Wisdom's Caravan:

Yeshua adds to his wisdom teaching about the process of finding with this simple admonition—chose not to be led or pushed, even when it seems dark and you feel blind. Trust your own process, your own discernment, and only then can you enter into the fortified city on the hill, or become a lamp that spreads its light, and a voice that calls out from the rooftops.

He seems to understand that we so easily give our trust to others, give up our ability to walk a path at our own pace and in our own time. As a model, we can see he embodied this idea of fearlessness, teaching in cities and in the wilds, in places of worship, and at the wedding feast. He was able to tread in places that were darkened to the priests and teachers of his day, trusting in the light within him to illuminate those liminal cliff edges. That is the deeper message of this logion and it is one that resonates through the whole text: stand fearlessly and own the wisdom you find—you will not fall then, even when the whole world is dark.

Ameyn.

The Eastern Parallels:

"Only two kinds of people can attain self-knowledge: those who are not encumbered at all with learning, that is to say, whose minds are not over-crowded with thoughts borrowed from others; and those who, after studying all the scriptures and sciences, have come to realize that they know nothing."

— Ramakrishna

"If you desire to be pure, have firm faith, and slowly go on with your devotional practices without wasting your energy in useless scriptural discussions and arguments. Your little brain will otherwise be muddled."

— Ramakrishna

Going Deeper:

If you have been deeply immersed in the Christian tradition, do you find it more difficult to hear the "inner" message these logia may be trying to disclose to you? Similar to naming something and thinking that we know it, sometimes when we hear familiar words with a different ear, a listening ear, we find fresh meanings. What has been the experience of this deep listening for you so far?

Summation:

To Find means to decline being pushed or led by others or "tradition" into the necessary dark places of our spiritual path.

Logion 35

"Yeshua says,

You cannot take
a strong man's house by force
unless first you bind
his hands and remove him."

The First Response:

I was reading Rilke today--
how he soared as high as angels in light,
but found God actually dwelled
in the inner darkness.
That's a path I've walked before,
able to name this tree of success,
that bird of hoped-for applause on the way
to what I thought was an open sky
to what I thought was security and freedom.

Words and concepts are seldom such precise things
after all.

Humbling to know that God was in the shadows,
watching it all
in amusement, I think.

Laughter cuts what ties us tight—
don't forget that.

There will be a time
when we are all bound
and pulled from our homes,

from these little lines and boundaries and expectations
we call,
so easily
"I"
and thrust into the larger
"I"
that is spacious, and free
and so dark our eyes will
ache with the beauty of it
and if we are lucky,
we
will,
all of us,
giggle.

Today in Wisdom's Caravan:

Violence laces through-out the words of wisdom
teachers, and Yeshua's sayings are no exception. They make
literal readers scratch their heads and mumble about
"inconsistencies" and "later additions to the canon" and such
things that force the sayings into their comfortable conceptual
boxes. But what house are they trying to protect when they do
this, in the way of the strong man or woman? Mostly, it is the
house that is called in western parlance "the ego."

Yeshua is actually asking us to *submit* to being bound
and removed. In "nicer" language, we call this surrender. It is
not a sign of weakness. Notice that the man (or woman) in the
logion is strong.

Whether it is the Tibetan bodhisattva Manjushri cutting
the bonds of ignorance with his flaming sword or Yeshua
metaphorically dragging the bound man beyond his imagined
boundaries of comfort and security, this is an intrinsic,
sometimes painful, and frightening part of *actually finding*. It is
also a warning that the spiritual path is not at all about shoring

up the ego, but in fact, dismantling it, pulling the ground out from beneath our feet and leaving us like naked children before the immensity of our truer self that is continuous with God.

After all, can you imagine God crammed into one small house? Are you not, as Emerson once wrote, "part and parcel of God" who is vast and timeless?

Ameyn.

The Eastern Parallels:

"One day, a fire broke out in the house of a wealthy man who had many children. The wealthy man shouted at his children inside the burning house to flee. But the children were absorbed in their games and did not heed his warning even though the house was being consumed by flames.

Then, the wealthy man devised a practical way to lure the children from the burning house. Knowing that the children were fond of interesting playthings, he called out to them, "Listen! Outside the gate are the carts that you have always wanted: carts pulled by goats, carts pulled by deer, and carts pulled by oxen. Why don't you come out and play with them?" The wealthy man knew that these things would be irresistible to his children.

The children, eager to play with these new toys rushed out of the house but, instead of the carts that he had promised, the father gave them a cart much better than any he had described - a cart draped with precious stones and pulled by white bullocks. The important point, however, was that the children were saved from the dangers of the house on fire."

The Parable of the Burning House
appears in Chapter 3 (the Hiyu Chapter)
of the Lotus Sutra.

Going Deeper:

As in my poem above, what shape do the walls of your house take on for you? What keeps you caged and egoic? Can you draw a picture for yourself that captures what holds and contains the small sense of yourself and what it might be like to be pulled from such a house and given the freedom that is your birthright?

Summation:

To Find means to be willing to be ousted from the "house" of our small egoic self so that we have room to "find" the spaciousness that is our truer Self.

Logion 36

Yeshua says,

**"Do not spend your time
from one day to the next
worrying about your
outer appearance, what you wear, and
what you look like."**

The First Response:

The picture was faded,
perfectly square,
and I
sat on a old horse simply named
Lady,
hair in pig-tails, bits loose and caught in my mouth,
striped pants and
polka-dot shirt,
the fat old mare,
sagging on one hip,
her black tail a brush stroke of blurred motion.

How relaxed the look on my face.
Do my muscles still remember
how to smile
like
that?

Today in Wisdom's Caravan:

This logion reflects the concept of the house of the ego,
but this time from the outside in—if Logion 34 was about the

157

experience of the Self bound within the confines of the small self, this is the picture of how we also wear societal masks in the form of dress and appearance to display the ego to the world. Both the inner walls and the outer masks contribute to make us feel alone, afraid, and judged.

It also takes tremendous energy to maintain both the walls and the masks, energy that could be spent in other more creative ways. The fire that is seeded into the cosmos is reduced to something personal, small and ultimately selfish. Notice Yeshua isn't saying, "don't dress carefully" or "don't take a bath, brush your teeth or wash your hair." Self-care at this level of reality is still important. Rather, he is pointing out that we spend a great deal of our time in *worry,* day after day. Worry is a form of trying to control a situation or an appearance, and Yeshua is asking us to question why we do this. In this country, such worry is the root of huge industries—makeup, apparel, tooth whiteners, slimming products, on and on. In a sense this fundamental fear is what drives most of our economy. Trace any advertising to its root emotion and you will find worry and fear at its base.

Yet, if we are part of the great I-I, the union with God, everything is already ours and basic self-care is part of the respect of the divine for the divine. That's all. It's that simple. And that confounding.

Ameyn.

The Eastern Parallels:

"Learn everything that is Good from Others, but bring it in, and in your own way absorb it; do not become others."

— Swami Vivekananda

"Be not afraid of anything. You will do marvelous work. It is fear that is the great cause of misery in the world. It is fear that is the greatest of all superstitions. It is fear that is the cause of all our woes, and it is fearlessness that brings heaven even in a moment. Therefore, "arise, awake and stop not until the goal is reached."

— Swami Vivekananda

"You find in Krishna that non-attachment is the central idea."

— Swami Vivekananda

Going Deeper:

It is very enlightening to keep an informal track how of much, in the course of a day, you think about or work at the appearance of yourself for appearance sake and not just the basic care of your body. If you feel called, jot down each time your mind turns this way. Do this practice in the spirit of humor or the scientific mood of just seeing how your mind works, not out of violence toward yourself. What did you find?

Summation:

To Find means to turn the energy of worrying about externals into the fire of internal creativity.

Logion 37

His students asked him,

"When will you manifest
your self to us?
How long will it be
before we see you as you truly are?"

Yeshua replied,

"On the day you strip yourselves naked like
little children
and trample your clothes on the ground under
your feet without shame,
then you will be able to look upon
the son of the Living One,
without fear."

The First Response:

I will see you when
you
see
me,
when the we-ness dissolves
and that naked place emerges,
where the pupil of the eye puddles and drips
backwards into the skull,
and that full darkness coats
everything that has a name,
when the one light
can't be seen because we are That,
mirror-less
in our rippling mystery.

Today in Wisdom's Caravan:

I like this image—when you are able to be naked so I can really see you without masks and artifice, then you will see me and that seeing will be free from projection, fear or any sense of "otherness". This is the capping moment of finding, when the disciple moves from walking behind to walking with his or her spiritual master in an attitude of trust and relationship. Or when we open this way to reality and God.

We can see how the logia have set us up for this moment, angle by angle, word by word. We can begin to see why Yeshua talked about a narrow path—he really defined it with a great deal of focus and clarity and even finding it requires a great deal of shedding our old ways of being in the world before we can even begin to understand that we have indeed "found" something worthwhile.

Ameyn.

The Eastern Parallels:

"I cannot stand anyone calling me guru. It irritates me. Who is the guru? Satchidananda alone is the guru.'
(Satchitananda=being, consciousness and bliss)."

--Ramakrishna

"Unless one always speaks the truth, one cannot find God Who is the soul of truth. One must be very particular about telling the truth. Through truth one can realize God."

--Ramakrishna

Going Deeper:

As you read slowly through the collected lines that complete this second section of the Gospel of Thomas, where do you find your greatest challenge to "finding" your spiritual path? What might you do to work with this challenge?

Summation:

To Find means to be brave enough to see our spiritual teachers without bias or artifice, freely seeing them as they see us.

Transition Logion 38

Yeshua says,

"On many occasions
you have longed
to hear such words as
the ones I am speaking to you,
but you had no one to go to.
The day will come again
when you will seek for me,
but you will not be able to find me."

The First Response:

I picked up bits of sea glass as I walked,
head bent,
in search of that elusive blue or green
amidst the barnacled shells
and fractured bits of water-soothed volcanoes.
It took a yell from my husband
for me to lift my head,
and OH!
A glorious arch of color footed itself
in the Sound,
its curve lost in blue skies

but its foundations defined by low, patchy clouds.

For one moment in time,
I'd seen the ends of the rainbow.

Today in Wisdom's Caravan:

If we are following Lynn Bauman's theoretical metaframe, that the Gospel of Thomas can be evenly distributed among the topics of searching, finding, trouble, wonder, reigning and rest, with a transition logion standing between each section, these words bear both an invitation and a warning.

The invitation is that if we put the "way" of Yeshua into practice, we will indeed find what we have been searching for, and that finding will bring up a sense of deep trouble for us. All the struggle that came before to see a new paradigm, a new way of being in relationship, a new way of working with both the material universe and the ephemeral "spirit" within us all will begin to snap into clear focus but throw everything we once believed into question.

The warning is simple—"you must *find* because if you are leaning me as your physical guide, I won't always be here. And that will lead you into deep and distressing Trouble. The teaching must be internalized; you must take a stand and proclaim to yourself that you have found a way to work with the world. That takes an incredible act of bravery and discernment. But then, any undertaking that promises to change our lives will of course require of us tremendous inner resources, a blend of heart and head, a huge helping of grace, and a kind of egoless allowing that is often the most difficult piece of all.

Trouble awaits us as we struggle to implement the implications of a new paradigm. It is a necessary stage, the mixed emotions of holding two paradigms at once for a time, and really beginning to see what discipleship means.

Ameyn.

The Eastern Parallels:

"I come to tell you all of Him,
and the way to encase Him in your bosom...

164

and yet when I am only a dream to you,
I will come to remind you that you, too, are naught
but a dream of my Heavenly Beloved;
and when you know you are a dream, as I know now,
we will be ever awake in Him."

-- Yogananda

"Tell me what kind of company a person keeps and I will tell you what he is. We always enjoy the company of those who flatter us, but this weakens us. We should prefer the company of those who tell us the truth and help us to be better. He is your best friend who humbly suggests to you how you may improve and benefit yourself. If we always live in the company of flatterers, it is bad for us--for our spiritual growth."

-- Yogananda

Going Deeper:

Close your eyes and breathe deeply into your belly. When you have settled, allow yourself to feel any places in your heart or belly or mind that feel heavy, frightened, or alone. Inhale and give those sensations your full attention. Exhale and send them a sense of companionship and acceptance. Breath by breath, continue this inner conversation without needing to change anything, run for help, or run away from yourself. Simply be "with".

Summation:

> *Transition: The work of Finding ripens still more when we encounter Trouble; Finding fulfills the deep mission of the spiritual guide, which is to create students who no longer need him or her as simply someone to follow, but who begin to come to their own feet and stand—but this can be deeply troubling to us.*

To Find means...

20 *to allow ourselves to be gifted with the smallest seeds of the great Tree of Life.*

21 *to be willing to see the ripening happening within ourselves that cannot be hurried or pressed into a human sense of completion.*

22. *to use the gifts of attention, creativity and will with a child's sense of belonging and place.*

23. *to fully recognize our unique sovereignty and utter interdependency with all of life.*

24. *to accept with full awareness that we are not called to merely worship, but rather, to Stand and shine forth who we were all created to be.*

25. *to preserve and cherish the larger community that helps us discern light.*

26. *to open to all of ourselves, including our shadows, so that we might be of discerning service to others.*

27. *to begin to suspect the division between the sacred and the profane, between the acts and concepts of religion and the life of the spirit.*

28. *to be willing to throw off our inebriation and stand up into both relative and ultimate reality.*

29. *to be willing to acknowledge with each breath we do not just exist for spirit—spirit also exists for us.*

30. *to be willing to claim the unifying divinity that under-girds the many and varied individuals.*

31. *to truly see the divinity in all those around you, transcending your own tendency to mask and objectify them.*

32. *to move beyond only observing life and into the pulsing energy of participation.*

33. *to be willing to share our discoveries, helping to create the bonds of relationship.*

34. *to decline being pushed or led by others or tradition into the necessary darkness of your spiritual path*

35. *to be willing to be ousted from the "house" of our small egoic self so that we have room to "find" the spaciousness that is our truer Self.*

36. *to turn the energy of worrying about externals into the fire of internal creativity.*

37. *to be brave enough to see our spiritual teachers without bias or artifice, freely seeing them as they see us.*

Transition (Logion 38): The work of Finding ripens still more when we encounter Trouble; finding fulfills the deep mission of the spiritual guide, which is to create students who no longer need him or her as simply someone to follow, but who begin to come to their own feet and stand—but this can be deeply troubling to us.

The Third Movement:
The Logia about Trouble

Logion 39

Yeshua says,

"Your scholars and religious leaders
have taken the keys
of knowledge and
locked them away.
They have not used them
to enter in, nor have they allowed those desiring
it to do so.
You, therefore, must be
as subtle as serpents and
as guileless as doves."

The First Response:

It's tedious to weed the labyrinth,
walk a few steps, winding
into some designated middle,
flick the bit of green
from its grip on reddish stone and
pocket it for the compost pile.
Every now and then I look up—
how much further
or worse
what's for lunch?
I swear the path in
is longer than the path out,
but maybe that's a good thing...
I laugh when I see a chickadee flit
over the lines and curves
and drop
gracefully into the center.
A moment's jitterbug and startle
and she is away again.

I used to color like that in kindergarten—
no respect for lines at all.

Today in Wisdom's Caravan:

Yeshua is incredibly sensitive to the power that the knowledge of reality holds—it can topple kingdoms, unseat the wealthy and lift the whole of humanity into relationship. One of the best ways to control any population and maintain personal wealth and power is to control information and knowledge. In this case, though, even the scholars and priests have not "entered in", not used the wealth and knowledge that is at their disposal to examine their own behaviors and ideologies. They have become the worst gate-keepers, blind to even what they are so rigidly guarding. This is one kind of trouble—the traditional ways to get at the truth are sometimes not "living ways" at all.

The technique of seeing into reality at the level of the heart requires us to stay earthy, with our belly's low to the ground, winding our way in a spiral that takes us to the core of what is hidden. Or, with wings of trust and grace, we might slip like a feathered arrow into the heart of truth. The snake and the dove are both paths that allow us to access knowledge in spite of the apparent blockade.

I am aware, too, that the serpent might hint at what guarded the Tree of Knowledge in Paradise and the dove was often a sacrifice at the temple. They are ways to gnosis that have their own shadow sides, and their use here may well be a warning about the trouble we will encounter as we begin to live into Finding. Many of the Trouble logia require us to practice a razor-edged discernment that can trigger overtones of loneliness or aggressiveness, depending upon our natures.

Ameyn.

The Eastern Parallels:

"He is the source of light in all luminous objects. He is beyond the darkness of matter and is unmanifested. He is knowledge, He is the object of knowledge, and He is the goal of knowledge. He is situated in everyone's heart."

--The Bhagavad-Gita

Going Deeper:

In what ways could the doors of knowledge be barred across your own heart by what you have learned from others? Rest lightly in meditation, breathing in a sense of light and breathing out your gift of light back to the world, imagining the doors to Truth swinging gently on loose hinges.

Summation:

Trouble arises in us when we begin to understand that what we thought were our sources for Searching and Finding Truth may contain their own agendas and immature understandings, and that we must approach the Truth more intuitively and on our own.

Logion 40

Yeshua says,

**"A grapevine was planted
away from its source
where it remains unprotected.
It will be torn out by its roots
and destroyed."**

The First Response:

From sun and rain cloud heaviness and wild wind,
from the faceless bits of things dead, decaying,
rocks coughed up from the deep,
mashed to become soil,
oxygen molecules and photosynthesis,
and an old leaning arbor,
rusted nails and peeling wood,
from vine to grape,
from grape to wine,
from wine to communion,
soaking bread and lips—
the secret question?
Where does resurrection begin
really?
And really,
where does it end?

Today in Wisdom's Caravan:

Pay attention whenever Yeshua speaks of grapevines.
You'll find that he is focusing on community, the broader
relationship we share with each other and Reality as such. He

172

seems to be saying here that when a community becomes cut off from its living and organic waters, it, like any organic and living entity, will be vulnerable.

If we compare many of our churches to his idea of the lonely grapevine, we can begin to catch the hints of trouble here. So often, we try to create a false world where our particular church or religion has the "right" understanding of God. That puts a community in a place that is cut off, isolated, and the stiffness of their position is the same stiffness of a dying plant. At its root, it is dying, and Yeshua notes it will be ripped out.

Our work, then, becomes inclusion and re-entry into the whole of Reality, something much harder to do within an institution of any kind by the way. Unless the group is made up of people who are able to stand and see beyond the confines of their belief, creeds and dogmas, it will always be a little vulnerable, a vine alone in the world.

Ameyn.

The Eastern Parallels:

"I am the thread that runs through all these pearls," and each pearl is a religion or even a sect thereof. Such are the different pearls, and God is the thread that runs through all of them; most people, however, are entirely unconscious of it."

--Vivekananda

"God is self-evident, impersonal, omniscient, the Knower and the Master of nature, the Lord of all. He is behind all worship and it is being done according to Him, whether we know it or not."

--Vivekananda

Going Deeper:

If you are part of a church community, can you identify the subtle ways that it separates itself out from the Source that is shared by all faiths? How might you work with this isolation and yet stay true to the roots of what you have personally experienced?

Summation:

Trouble arises when communities, thinking they have the "only" view of reality, become cut off from their shared and abundant Source.

Logion 41

Yeshua says,

*"To the one who has
something in hand,
more will be given.
To the one whose hands hold nothing
even that 'nothing' will be taken away."*

The First Response:

There are magnetic days,
the world-filings cutting my hands
and bowing my shoulders with I-beams.
They started as attractive burdens
but now, I don't know how to put it all down.
I wonder how the nothing of nothing feels,
the mind-bending zero state
when I even have to give away my breath
and finally enter into the lightness of the universe
weightless in word and being
at last.

Today in Wisdom's Caravan:

This is a fascinating logion because it could be one of those "flip" experiences where something and nothing are played off each other. Perhaps the have more-want more material culture is really the one experiencing the burdens of "more" and the empty hands freed from the acquisition of even spiritual experiences are finally introduced to a non-dual and non-conceptual place that is ironically the state of greatest fullness. That's where my poetry took me today, a place of kenosis or emptying in order to receive something that could not be added to the ego-tally of my life.

It's the like the Zen master refusing to teach a student whose mind is already too full of concepts or the image Yeshua uses in his teachings of the children stripping off their clothes and standing without masks, possessions, power, or identity.

And this is deeply troubling to us. Who are we without the things, the identities, the expectations? It throws us back on the classic Indian question of Ramana Maharshi: "Who are you? Who are you really?" Do you have the courage to stand in that kind of nakedness and seek the true answer? And once you have found it, what will it take to live out of that knowledge? Nothing. Everything. Exactly.

Ameyn.

The Eastern Parallels:

"What is illusion?
M.: To whom is the illusion? Find it out. Then illusion will vanish. Generally people want to know about illusion and do not examine to whom it is. It is foolish. Illusion is outside and unknown. But the seeker is considered to be known and is inside. Find out what is immediate, intimate, instead of trying to find out what is distant and unknown."

— Ramana Maharshi

Going Deeper:

"If you are able to give yourself a gift of a day of silence, practice this deep asking of "who am I?" Notice what happens when the roles, expectations, relationships, and everything we have acquired with education, money, up-bringing, and our religion of origin is stripped away. What is the antidote to the "trouble" of this work?"

Summation:

Trouble arises when we are faced with the kenosis that spiritual "finding" demands of us.

Logion 42

Yeshua says,

"Come into being
as you pass
away."

The First Response:

What editors of life we tend to be,
adding the brush of highlights to good memories,
squirreling away the shadows at the back of closets,
giving the bad experience the sanctifying spin of lessons
learned,
categorizing, objectifying,
everything piled up on the shoulders of a weighty
"I".

Editors are experiencers of an experiencer's experience.

What, then, is *being*?
Take ten breaths
after
this
period.

Today in Wisdom's Caravan:

This logion tends to clarify the one that came before. It
shows us that Yeshua is much more about taking things, ideas
and self concepts out of our hands, rather than adding to them,
much more concerned with the act of kenosis or self-emptying
than beefing up the ego. I find myself actually writing this

during the season of Lent, and the words go very well with the mood of this liturgical time.

The trouble we encounter here is all about the practice of getting out of the way of ourselves. This sort of deep surrender to "nothing" at all, in other words, to practice surrendering for surrendering's sake, is very foreign to most of us. Yeshua is in fact waiting for us to make the leap, to embrace that moment when we understand that the "nothing" we find is a great and brilliant fullness. We come into true "being" even as our past and future slip away. We find, in the parlance of the last few years, our Now. In that place we realize that even our spiritual beliefs and practices must be recognized as the simple metaphors they are before a nameless and vast Mystery.

Ameyn.

The Eastern Parallels:

"Even as fire finds peace in its resting place without fuel, when thoughts become silence, the soul finds peace in its own source. When the mind is silent, then it can enter into a world which is far beyond the mind, the highest End. The mind should be kept in the heart as long as it has not reached the highest End. This is wisdom, and this is liberation."

--The Upanishads

"Knowledge of the Divine dissolves all bonds and gives freedom from every kind of misery including birth and death."

--S'vetasvatara Upanishad

Going Deeper:

Today, simply following your breath in and out, allow it to find its own rhythm as you track it with your mind. When your mind is more quiet, simply sit and accept what your senses bring you without labeling or judging. Allow yourself to feel the spaciousness of simply being.

Summation:

Trouble arises when we realize that to "be" we have to move into the holy present moment, releasing all the burdens of egoic clinging.

Logion 43

His students said to him,

"Who are you to
be saying
such things to us?"

Yeshua replied,

"Do you not realize who I am
from everything I have said to you?
Have you come to be like the Judeans
who either accept the tree
but reject its fruit, or welcome the fruit
and despise the tree?"

The First Response:

If you were to meet
a famous movie star,
who would you really see?
What myriad and fanciful characters would you reference
in your mind,
draping them like veils
over the real human
before you?
Now imagine you met
this man called Jesus—
before
you knew him as
the face of God.
Before you knew he would die
on a cross.

Before the Gospels and letters were written,
crafting your "knowledge" of him,
thousands of veils thrown over his face—
today,
everyday
watch carefully the people who flow around you
for we walk elbow to elbow with divinity
and do
not
see.

Today in Wisdom's Caravan:

How often do we craft, in our minds, "who" our friends should be, based on our past experiences with them? Or what happens when we "meet" people through their art, their profound thoughts, their political face? Do we think we know "who" they are? Yeshua is aware of this very human fallibility of ours—a small, shy high school friend could surely not run for state governor, nor could that famous love poet scream at his family dog. We think we can keep the tree and shake our head at the fruits, or take the fruit and deny the tree. We have more control this way. We think we possess the whole Truth.

If we apply the wisdom in this logion to Yeshua himself, as he is clearly asking his disciples to do, we might find ourselves shaken. The question of "who are you" is profound, in all its nuances. Through-out his teaching career, there were those who could not hear Yeshua's message because they knew him as "Mary's son" and other times when people could not see "Mary's son" because of his profound teachings and healings. Either act objectifies, and either act gives us only a partial glimpse into the full personhood of Yeshua or anyone else for that matter.

The ramification of discipleship that is called into this full seeing means trouble with a capital "T". Suddenly, we are called by this Gospel to hold the *whole* person before us, no matter what their face or name, and to see the fleshy divinity that is the entire majesty of any living thing. We are thrown back on our own resources again, asked to see more than this particular teacher and his words, but at the same time, more than this fallible human being who could not possibly utter or manifest anything of value. We are called to do this not just in Yeshua's case, but for all those around us, creating sacred relationship out of our "finding".

Ameyn.

The Eastern Parallels:

"Bondage and Liberation are of the mind alone."

— Ramakrishna

"God is everywhere, but He is most manifest in man. So serve man as God. That is as good as worshipping God."

— Ramakrishna

"When divine vision is attained, all appear equal, and there remains no distinction of good and bad, or of high and low."

— Ramakrishna

Going Deeper:

The Buddhist tradition has a lovely practice of secretly wishing each person you brush by a sense of happiness, freedom from suffering and from the causes of suffering. Make your own words today that serve as a way to connect with people in deep compassion, and as you go about your day, offer them soundlessly to whoever catches your eye. At the end of the day, evaluate how you yourself feel when you bless others.

Summation:

Trouble arises when we do not recognize the "fleshy divinity" of each living thing, including our spiritual masters and furthest stranger.

Logion 44

Yeshua says

*"You may speak against the Father
and it will be forgotten.
You may speak against the son and it
will be dropped.
But if you speak opposing
the sacred Spirit,
that is irrevocable
both in heaven and on earth."*

The First Response:

Speak, then the things that are
crafted from speech,
and play with them all
like a child, tossing
wondering,
dreaming,
anchoring,
rebel against them,
cast them away,
it will not matter.
But hold close the first brush
with the song,
the shape that flits across the sun-ray,
the sigh of some white curve
rushing up on the beach—
hold close the world
before it rushes
into word and concept
into yes and
no.

Today in Wisdom's Caravan:

The Father and Son are simply concepts we've created in our mind, thought-forms to hold a steady sense of God as we face the impossible immensity that is truly the Divine, Ultimate Reality, etc. All religions do it to a point, create something concrete in shape or word that mediates our contact with the Mystery. But, as in the Tao te Ching's first lines, "The name that can be named is not the Name" or the Jewish tradition of not uttering the name of God, we must not speak out against the Spirit because we *cannot*. We can only play conceptually with what we bring into concrete forms of words or numbers or images, and these things are not God as IT IS or I AM THAT I AM.

This is a profound teaching, a deep teaching, about how we work with reality in our minds, filtering and naming and thinking again that we somehow know and control and have made "safe" something so vast that we truly should stand in awe, utterly speechless and beyond the concept-creating mind. And that is the trouble, because we want to be in relationship, we want to be able to grasp and hold and dance with that immensity.

Yeshua isn't saying that the concepts of Father and Son aren't lovely and useful—he's saying they are *not all there is to the Mystery*. You can deny the package that humankind creates for the Divine, but you cannot deny the Presence that is timeless, infinite, and infusing everything in a way un-named and un-defined.

Ameyn.

The Eastern Parallels:

"It is not the language but the speaker we want to understand."
--The Upanishads

"The self-existent Lord pierced the senses to turn outward. Thus we look to the world outside and see not the Self within us. A sage withdrew his senses from the world of change and, seeking immortality, looked within and beheld the deathless self."

--Katha Upanishad

Going Deeper:

Today, you might try to draw something in your environment, just looking at its shape, its textures and the way light plays over its surface. Avoid naming—just see it. Don't worry if you aren't an artist—just see.

Summation:

Trouble arises when we name something to come into relationship with it, only to find we find we have tried to concretize infinity.

Logion 45

Yeshua says,

"Grapes are not
harvested from thorns,
nor are figs gathered from
thistles—neither produce fruit.

Good people
bring goodness out of
a storehouse of inner treasure,
while evil ones bring wickedness
out of the repository of evil
collected in the heart.
It is from there that they speak.
For from the heart's overflow,
evil enters the world."

The First Response:

He tried to whisper it a thousand times
because he could not say it out-loud:
go out into the desert alone,
smile gently on the stranger,
sit at the wedding feast and
turn mere water into wine with your generosity,
feed people fish and bread,
allow yourself to be changed,
heal with no sense of reward,
tell the truth,
no, not the one someone wrote down
and people recite without hearing,
but rather
the truth of deep and abiding

relationship.
If only we could grasp
we do not initially change our minds
or act in the world--
first,
we change our hearts.

Today in Wisdom's Caravan:

Vietnamese Buddhist teacher Thich Nhat Hahn often teaches about seed consciousness, the idea that the seeds we water in our hearts, be those our darker and more selfish impulses or our more noble and compassionate ones, will be the seeds that grow out and manifest in our very thoughts and actions. And as the thought or action, so the fruit and seeds we may help to plant in others.

As we speak and do good, we actually reinforce the good in ourselves and those we touch. We are, in a sense, cultivating the organic nature of the heart and mind in a way to vouchsafe the positive energy of relationship. Our work is not to "believe" in our spiritual Master, but come to be *like* him at the level of our hearts. The first movement is easy, the second, incredibly troubling and hard because we must not just be able to say the right words, we must show our understanding through the way we relate with our world.

Grapes and figs are the ties that bind us to community, food held in common, food that links us back to the vine and tree from which it came and all of creation that supports it, food that is passed hand to hand in communion with one another. The thorn and the thistle tear and rend and separate. Yes, both trees are still "of God" but the sharp-edged ones are more lonely, and less able to enter into the deeper transformation of ripeness from tree to flesh to consciousness. As metaphor, they suffer in their aloneness, the crown of thorns cutting them off, one from another.

Ameyn.

The Eastern Parallels:

"No one who does good work will ever come to a bad end, either here or in the world to come."

— The Bhagavad-Gita

"Our practice is based on the insight of non-duality—anger is not an enemy. Both mindfulness and anger are ourselves. Mindfulness is there not to suppress or fight against anger, but to recognize and take care of it—like a big brother helping a younger brother. So the energy of anger is recognized and embraced tenderly by the energy of mindfulness."

--Thich Nhat Hanh
March 2011 Shambala Sun

Going Deeper:

You might enjoy reading a rule of life, like the Rule of St. Benedict, which is really about cultivating the good seeds of community life. Give it a try and journal a bit about what you resonate with.

Summation:

Trouble arises when we realize that every thought and action adds to the granary of relationship or isolation, each creating its own fruit in time.

Logion 46

Yeshua says,

"Among those born on earth
beginning from Adam to
John the Baptist,
no one has reached a higher state
than John—and you should
bow in honor before him.

Yet I tell you this,
whoever of you becomes "a little child"
will not only know the kingdom,
but will be raised to a state
higher than John's."

The First Response:

Have you touched the river's surface
with your fingertips,
lifted them dripping and stared
as ripples elongated and swirled
into currents
and
liquid settings for smooth black stones?
What shadow of forgetfulness
that you dragged through blackberry patches
and over slippery moss,
in that moment,
washed away,
dancing with sunlight on the rapids?
With each breath,
we baptize ourselves,
continuously renewed in

childlike
reverence.

Today in Wisdom's Caravan:

John could not give people the awakened sense of the spirit around and within them, only dip them into the cold, rushing waters and shock them for that one moment, reminding them of their first breath as a baby. Each breath we take can be like that—purely aware of that simplest sip of oxygen. John is honored the way a Rinzai Zen master is honored for compassionately pushing his student into the pond. He pushed at the perfect moment, yes, but the student him or herself has to actually awaken, that moment and every moment after.

The student who maintains that awareness, though, is not simply in a "state", which is static. The baptismal awareness flows; it is organic, skillful, and timeless. As such, it transcends the "one way" of awakening and sees each moment as a dip in the river. In this way, the student even transcends the "way" of John and has found his or her own Way.

It's troubling, though, to believe that our spiritual teachers themselves must be seen as the temporary guides they are. And it is troubling, too, to realize just how easy and just how world-changing living into what we have found and who we really are can be.

Ameyn.

The Eastern Parallels:

"Faith is realization itself. It harbors no destructive element, as does belief. Belief can be swayed or destroyed by contrary evidence and doubt, but faith is ever secure, because it is direct perception of truth. Once the world was believed to be flat, but with the progress of science it was found to be round, so that was only a belief which had to be given up. But faith cannot be contradicted, for it is the developed expression of the unerring intuition within us, which brings us face to face with theretofore unseen realities. One may thus rightly refer to blind belief, but not blind faith."

--Yogananda

"Self-realization is the knowing – in body, mind, and soul – that we are one with the omnipresence of God; that we do not have to pray that it come to us, that we are not merely near it at all times, but that God's omnipresence is our omnipresence; that we are just as much a part of Him now as we ever will be. All we have to do is improve our knowing."

--Yogananda

Going Deeper:

Write down three people you respect and admire. Then, list the traits in them that cause you to admire them. Now, on a separate piece of paper, write down the traits you most admire in yourself. Compare the two lists—see anything interesting?

Summation:

Trouble arises when we begin to understand that we are called to live beyond our spiritual teachers by simply being ourselves and fully conscious.

Logion 47

Yeshua says,

"No one can mount two horses
or draw two bows at once,
and you cannot serve
two masters at the same time.
If you honor one,
the other will be offended.

No one drinks a vintage wine
and immediately wants
wine freshly bottled.
New wine is not put into
old containers lest it be ruined,
nor is aged wine put into
new barrels lest it spoil.

Also, old cloth is not sewn
onto new garments because
it only makes the tear worse."

The First Response:

Sometimes,
we mistake our own narrow path
for the only one,
the best one.
And that's because maybe it is
for us.
Still,
I lived in a woods riddled with paths,
some wide and crafted two-tracks,
some the deer tramped

194

on their way to living water.
I've walked them all
and really
any of them are easier
than tripping
through the bracken and ankle-deep mud.
Sooner or later,
they all get to the river
or the asphalt.

But when you are really turned around and lost,
the light shadowing the trees,
the cold pinching your nose shut,
the darkened forest rustle startling you,
I hope you have a compass or GPS,
magnetic north or satellites,
something
with
the
bigger
picture
that can lead you home.

Today in Wisdom's Caravan:

Paradigm change of any kind is troublesome. For a while, we try to do a kind of parallel processing—use the old system as we try the new system out. It's twice as much work and in the end, not only inefficient, but rather frustrating and confusing. Yeshua has captured such a moment here—how to honor a new way of seeing the world as you let the old way go.

He seems to understand that humans cannot parallel process very well—riding two horses, serving two masters, sewing a new patch on old cloth all speak to this discomfort, the kind of split in our personality. And the fine old wine is simply better than the new wine, that is, until the new has a chance to age and come into its own special nuances and flavors, much like a person on a fresh spiritual path.

Some might see all of this as the process and trouble of choosing one particular religion, but all through the Gospel of Thomas, Yeshua has been making it clear that he isn't talking about traditional religions here. He's speaking of THAT which informs all religions, the Mystery beyond this container, that piece of clothing, that dogma or form we paste on God. When we lift our eyes to the bigger picture, or if you prefer, to the ground of all our being, then we find ourselves on a wholly different path indeed.

Ameyn.

The Eastern Parallels:

"On this path no effort is wasted,
no gain is ever reversed;
even a little of this practice
will shelter you from great sorrow."

--The Bhagavad-Gita

"The light breaking upon the mind should not be excluded by that false logic which puts forth unholy guesses of every kind up to the obliteration even of the facts of consciousness."

--Yogavasishtha

Going Deeper:

When have you experienced a paradigm change in your own life? Can you remember believing in Santa Claus and then learning he was more the "spirit" of Christmas than an actual being? How did that feel? What other times have you shifted from one way of "knowing" to another?

Summation:

Troubles arises when we try to hold two competing spiritual paradigms at once—faith as the product of a culturally conditioned institution or faith as inner experience—and we must choose which path to follow.

Logion 48

Yeshua says,

"Should two make peace
in one house,
they could speak the word,
"Move!" to a mountain,
and it would obey them."

The First Response:

Groaning, it sighs in dust and stone at last,
lifts itself off the continental shelf
and jumps a little, testing the air
before it floats upward.
The pines on its slope shiver,
the bears grab hold of them, point their black snouts
skyward.
Rivers pours off its edges, falling on the flat land,
cutting in,
wild new patterns,
living water,
while the eagle hovers on a parallel updraft,
amazed and amused in turn:
someone must have awakened somewhere,
unified within,
and called
a
mountain
to them...
again.

Today in Wisdom's Caravan:

I couldn't help the poem that bubbled up today. The image was so delightfully impossible, a flashback to the floating mountains in the movie *Avatar*. I just wanted to bathe in it for a moment, looking up at a mountain taking flight. And yet, our big institutions are like mountains in some senses—seemingly immovable, hierarchical in their structure, cold sometimes, with spirit flitting around and only occasionally landing. There are other mountainous metaphors as well—oppression, illness, greedy political structures, our own hatreds and fears and worries. If we are unified within, each of us can be the fulcrum that moves such mountains.

And what does it mean when two make peace in one house? I believe Yeshua is pointing to the house of our body, and the two lenses through which we see the world—the dualistic or relative view that we absolutely must use to function in the world and the non-dualistic view that allows us to see the sacred in everything, to see the system and relationship that is always present in the relative as well.

Yeshua himself demonstrates this. Think what mountains he has continued to move even after his physical death, his spirit gliding through countless millions. Once again, a saying does not have to be factual to be true. The trouble is, we don't believe in our strength, even at the metaphorical level. We keep ourselves small and weak, something Yeshua is trying to gently shake from us, like nudging a child out of sleep.

Ameyn.

The Eastern Parallels:

"Don't look backward but go forward, infinite energy, infinite enthusiasm, infinite daring, and infinite patience then alone can great deeds be accomplished."

--Swami Vivekananda

Going Deeper:

Part of what Yeshua is conveying here is the energy that is available to us when we are not, in ourselves, a house divided. Take up a writing instrument today and write down the ways you spend your energy internally—what are your worries, your fears, your great dreams, your daily lists of things to do. These are your mountains. Then consider what might happen if you could set aside much of what doesn't "matter" and turn yourself toward one great affirmation for the world, the one thing for which you were created. What is that one thing to you?

Summation:

Trouble arises when, even as we hold relative and ultimate reality within ourselves, we doubt the inner strength it gives to us.

Logion 49

Yeshua says,

"Blessed are those
chosen and unified.
The Realm of
the Kingdom is theirs.
For out of her you have come,
and back to her you are returning."

The First Response:

It is one thing to move mountains,
quite another to choose,
instead,
to fall
into the open arms
of black bamboo and cloud-scudded skies,
of spring ponds and the feathers of mallard ducks,
of the low murmur of the sheep punctuated
by the hawk's bright cry.
That's the deepest paradox of life--
knowing when to lift and when to put down,
knowing
you can move mountains
and
sometimes
choosing to gaze
and
be
moved.

Today in Wisdom's Caravan:

One of the delightful things about the Gospel of Thomas is the alternating of powerful, warrior kinds of energy with a gentler, allowing, gardener-kind of being. That sort of literary breathing, this action/non-action, forceful/allowing, speaking/listening is the very rhythm of our bodies and of relationship with our larger world. Day and night, work and rest—it's implicit in the very fabric of how we live.

The ashes-to-ashes and dust-to-dust trajectory of our lives is cast in a new light, too. We go from light to light, not so much dust to dust. The positive, continual life energy that we participate in, including the kingdom which language scholar Neil Douglas-Klotz has corrected to be "queendom" in Aramaic, is both our source and our end, our beginning and our destiny.

There is a warning here as well, coming fast on the heels of that ability to move mountains in logion 48. We catch a couple strange usages: the "realm" of the Kingdom of Heaven isn't a realm at all in most of the Gospel of Thomas, rather, it's a state of being. So why use it here? Perhaps it reminds us again that "form is emptiness and emptiness is form".

Also, "chosen" is a word we might stick on, until we again see that the very word makes us pause and consider this: *Who does the choosing?* Perhaps one way to see this is that "chosen" might be equated with "grace". *We wake up* in a way that makes us feel our blessedness and at the same time, we know it is available to each and very one of us. To be chosen is *to feel* in your gut the aliveness of the unitive state that Yeshua is pointing toward.

In a sense, these two pauses—*realm* and *chosen*--both ground us. They bind us back into relationship, shifting us from the individualistic "power that moves mountains" to a reminder that we are not separate from the world, but rather our Ultimate Source that is continuous *with* the world. To be unified is not to deny the beauty of this embodied self nor lose sight of the caravan of life of which we are a part. It is to hold the relative and the ultimate forms of reality easily, in communion, in a way that is blessed indeed.

Ameyn.

The Eastern Parallels:

"The man who sees me in everything
and everything within me
will not be lost to me, nor
will I ever be lost to him.

He who is rooted in oneness
realizes that I am
in every being; wherever
he goes, he remains in me.

When he sees all being as equal
in suffering or in joy
because they are like himself,
that man has grown perfect in yoga."

--The Bhagavad-Gita

Going Deeper:

What does the word "chosen" mean to you? Would you react differently to being "chosen" than to being a recipient of grace? Why or why not? What about the "realm of Heaven" rather than heaven as a state of being? Which resonates more with you today?

Summation:

Trouble arises when we begin to recognize that the Kingdom is not a realm at all, and that any sense of being "chosen" begs the question: "who is the chooser?"

Logion 50

Yeshua says,

"Suppose you are asked,
'Where have you come from?'
say, 'We have come from the
Light at its source,
from the place where it came forth
and was manifest as Image and Icon.'

If you are asked,
'Are you that Light?'
say, 'We are its children,
and chosen by the Source,
the Living Father.'

If you are questioned,
'But what is the sign of
the Source within you?'
say, 'It is movement and it is rest.'"

The First Response:
If I lay long enough in the sun,
seeing the pink tissue of my eyelids backlit,
the grass curling through and around my fingers,
I would be like the moth that flew
headlong into the flame,
nothing left.
But maybe we are called to something different,
a narrower path than extinction in ecstasy,
because,
my dog's wet tongue just slathered my hot cheek,
and sitting up,
a crow watches me from the shadows,

her silvered eye blinks,
open, shut
and then
she wings her way
through the brilliance.

Today in Wisdom's Caravan:

This is a very dense saying, so we'll unpack it a bit, section by section. First, we are introduced to the idea of image and icon. These two terms are critical if we are to understand Yeshua's teachings about masks, identity, isolation vs. community and the dance of relative and ultimate reality. An *image* is simply a thought-form, a sign if you will, that stands in for us or for anyone we are objectifying. It's not false, simply not the whole picture. It is what we project to the world and the projection we in turn force onto the cosmos. An *icon*, on the other hand, is a window into the divine that transcends the idea of an image; we see not only the outer meaning, but the inner aliveness as well. Notice that Light manifests as both—the material universe that we name, the signs we pay attention to like stop lights, the "ten thousands things" of relative reality. Yet, it also manifests as the icon, which catches the inner sacred light of the relative in a way that binds everything back to the source, the system, the Ultimate form of reality.

Now we find the word "chosen" again and we finally see what we are chosen *for*—to be both images and icons, to be that place where the sacred meets the material and we find they are not two at all.

And once again, we find the lovely wu-wei (action-in-non-action) tone of Yeshua's teaching—rise and fall, light and dark, image and icon, life and death. The Source is always "both/and" rather than "either/or". The Source is that in which we "live and move and have our being."

This then is both the wonderful news and the trouble. Because the very language used to define who we are, what our

Source is and the nature of its actions, will always be the language of process and paradox—not realms, signs and concrete forms and also nothing other than signs, realms, concrete forms when seen as the Icons they are.

Ameyn.

The Eastern Parallels:

"Body is nothing more than emptiness,
emptiness is nothing more than body.
The body is exactly empty,
and emptiness is exactly body.
The other four aspects of human existence --
feeling, thought, will, and consciousness --
are likewise nothing more than emptiness,
and emptiness nothing more than they.
All things are empty:
Nothing is born, nothing dies,
nothing is pure, nothing is stained,
nothing increases and nothing decreases."

--Heart Sutra, translation found on
http://webspace.ship.edu/cgboer/heartsutra.html

Going Deeper:

Look up and read the entire Heart Sutra today—it's not long, if that will be enough of a carrot. Do you find any resonance there with the words in the logion above?

Summation:

Trouble arises within us when we realize we will only be able to comprehend or verbally express to others what we have found in the language of process and paradox.

Logion 51

His students asked him,

"When does rest for
the dead begin
and when will the new
cosmos arrive?"

Yeshua replied,
"What you are looking for is already here.
You simply have not recognized it."

The First Response:

I dare you—
ask a question that isn't about the past
or anticipating the future, and every time
I bet you'll find
you've entered into relationship.
No, I don't just mean
the question itself,
a bridge of words
trying to straddle the gulf
of who we are, what we knew and will come to know,
but rather,
notice how it *feels*,
asking with the mind rooted in the now.
Because it's never the question itself,
but rather, the open-eared intent
that is
not anticipating
any specific answer
that will hear
into
the Source.

Today in Wisdom's Caravan:

It's already here, right now, this moment. The Kingdom (or Queendom) is blooming with every breath we take if we make the choice to see. Yeshua's been saying that, over and over, parable after parable, answering questions that touch its edges, living it for his disciples to see, and still they are asking the words and not listening to his responses in a deep way.

This is the trouble with finding *what we did not expect to find*. Our whole lives, many of us have been told religion is about behaviors, prophecies, creeds, dogmas, and realms that are concrete and somehow "other" than the lands and lives we now inhabit. The disciples wanted concrete answers that fit in with what they understood the religious path to be. Until we comprehend the deep divide between the paradigm that births the questions asked by those ancient disciples and the answers that Yeshua provides them, we miss the entire point.

My father used to tell me that to learn something, we must hear it 17 times and better yet, in 17 different ways. (He was an educator—can you tell?) If there are times when we become impatient with the disciples, perhaps we should remember my father's teaching as well as the incredibly difficult message Yeshua was trying to convey.

Ameyn.

The Eastern Parallels:

"As long as I live, so long do I learn."

--Ramakrishna

Going Deeper:

Today, you might try to draw a picture that illustrates the difference between an "idea" and a "paradigm" (how an idea is framed in its larger sense) or between an image and an icon. What did you learn from this work?

Summation:

Trouble arises within us when we realize that the new paradigm we are asked to adopt is not what most people expect to find when they begin the spiritual search.

Logion 52

His students said,

"Each of Israel's
twenty-four prophets
spoke about you."

Yeshua said,

"You ignore the one living in your
presence and talk only about the dead."

The First Response:

There are times when the words fail,
no wisdom in the past,
no expectations of a future,
and I can only touch the holes on my flute,
breathing through them
what sorrows and joys have short-circuited
the cement logic centers in my mind,
eyes closed,
tiny rays of light sneaking into the carved instrument
getting mixed up with O2 and spare change,
emerging just loud enough
that the beaver cutting through the first cattail shoots
drums his one-beat response--
a flat tail hitting the water
as he dives into his own
mystery.

Today in Wisdom's Caravan:

Comparisons are fine as far as they go, but it's always important to understand that when we compare one thing to another, one person to another, it's like taking a picture of a picture of a living being. Worse, if we conflate the picture with the living being in our minds, everything organic, unexpected, non-traditional and alive will freeze in that moment.

Comparison is also a slippery slope, causing us to make an image or sign that cannot respond in any creative way but also locks the object we have made out of someone into a set of responses that can then be evaluated and judged. Is this not part of what sent Yeshua to the cross, this inability of those in power to see that the holy is always organic, without walls, breaking through gender and race and politics? How painful it must have been for Yeshua to hear these words coming from his disciples, those closest to him.

Why would they do this? It's a natural and human response to change—review what you know and place the new information in the file that best fits it. If you can do that, you think you know it and it will create ground for you, even if the ground itself is conceptual and illusory. And because it is a human reaction, surely this must have been what kept Yeshua struggling to teach his Way right up to the very end of his physical life.

Ameyn.

The Eastern Parallels:

"Your duty is to be and not to be this or that. 'I am that I am' sums up the whole truth. The method is summed up in the words 'Be still'. What does stillness mean? It means destroy yourself. Because any form or shape is the cause for trouble. Give up the notion that 'I am so and so'. All that is required to realize the Self is to be still. What can be easier than that?"

--Ramana Maharshi

Going Deeper:

Music is a powerful medium because of its ability to bypass language and concept and speak directly to our hearts. What music speaks of non-dual consciousness to you?

Summation:

Trouble arises within us when we retreat into the dualistic mind of comparison in order to create a safe and familiar sense of ground.

Logion 53

His students asked him,

*"Is circumcision of
any help to us?"*

Yeshua replied,

*"If it were, your fathers would have
been born fully circumcised
from their mother's womb.
The only circumstance that will benefit
you at all is spiritual."*

The First Response:

There are times
when I have been enough—
leaning up against a horse in a fresh-cleaned stall,
watching little goats bounce like popcorn
thrown out from an open fire,
feeding my baby in shadow and moonlight,
watching my brother throw a fast-ball,
his eyes narrowed and intent.
Other times I've stopped up my holes,
with wadded spiritual texts,
felt like I needed to add some more letters behind my name,
or let myself get swept up
in church politics—
I won't make a long list,
because
you have your own,
all the little ways we say
the way God made us

is

not

quite

enough.

Today in Wisdom's Caravan:

I like the snarky Yeshua—there are a few logia scattered throughout the Gospel of Thomas that are so tongue-in-cheek that I, even across the thousands of years, hear him chuckling. Humor is a lovely way to teach, and he makes good use of it here as in other places (see especially logion 114) as a way to not just lighten the mood, but to shift consciousness. A Buddhist might call this sort of teaching a form of *upaya*, or skillful means. Laughter heals in the way that a serious discussion seldom can, and is yet another way to guide his students away from doing the "right" thing and into a wider understanding.

The word *benefit* is a tricky one; Yeshua has been at pains to show that it is the ego that cares about such things, stacking up wealth, looking good and "right". He may again be subtly pointing to the spiritual materialism that his students are mired in. While this word choice may be more about the sensitivity of the translator than Yeshua's actual intent, this marker works effectively here.

Finally, I enjoy the essential "suchness" of the cosmos that Yeshua points to, that we are blessed and fine just the way we are formed. No water, no knife, no special ritual or judgment from political or religious powerbrokers can improve on what God has created us to be.

Ameyn.

214

The Eastern Parallels:

"Dare to be free, dare to go as far as your thought leads, and dare to carry that out in your life. "

--Vivekananda

"The greatest sin is to think yourself weak."

--Vivekananda

Going Deeper:

In what ways do you try to prove you are enough in God's eyes? Where does this impulse come from? How might you live differently?

Summation:

Trouble arises when we think that by engaging in socially mandated rituals, we will deepen our understanding of the Kingdom of Heaven.

Logion 54

Yeshua says,

"You poor are blessed,
for the realm of heaven
is already yours."

The First Response:

Blessed
used to mean
whole and ripe,
not necessarily
rich or endowed or happy even,
but that deep-in-the bones
knowing
that everything is fair in the end
and in the middle
and at the beginning point—
a belief in a kind of foundation
that will never be
purely
ground.

Today in Wisdom's Caravan:

Whole and ripe, that's what blessed means to me. And poor here? It's something beyond the material. It's like the space that creates meaning within the walls of a jar, or the space between the spokes that forms the wheel as the Tao te Ching points out. It means being willing to let go of the branch because there is nothing material to cling to anymore, no false self to work so hard to maintain. Being poor is being exquisitely in free fall—no ground, no stored up grace, just the very face of being.

The word poor might also refer to the dark night of the soul, when we are stripped of meaning, consolation, and ego. To be poor means to be ever awake; each penny is meaningful, each mouthful of bread meaning-filled for eating is more than just satisfying our taste buds. It is a state that we can experience even if our bank account is very full, our job secure, our life deeply abundant in the ways of the world. We call it mindfulness, but it is very, very empty of expectation and evaluation.

Ameyn.

The Eastern Parallels:

"Remain still, with the conviction that the Self shines as everything yet nothing, within, without, and everywhere."

--Ramana Maharshi

"Realization is not acquisition of anything new nor is it a new faculty. It is only removal of all camouflage."

--Ramana Maharshi

Going Deeper:

What kinds of "positive poverty" are present within yourself? Draw them or write about them, bringing them into a grateful consciousness.

Summation:

Trouble arises within us when we face the tension between the very real grace of our "spiritual poverty" rather than the false nature of "spiritual materialism".

Logion 55

Yeshua says,

"Whoever does not
refuse father and mother
cannot be my student.
Whoever does not reject
brother and sister,
accepting the cross as I do,
is not ready for me."

The First Response:

Perhaps,
it's a survival instinct—
to wrap ourselves 'round with blankets
of family, tribe, church, nation.
Maybe one day, it'll even be
this world over another--
like we try to do with heaven
and
earth.

Today in Wisdom's Caravan:

In the very beginning of the *Bhagavad-Gita*, Arjuna the
warrior asks his charioteer to drive him between two great
armies. In this liminal space, he finally sees the faces of
grandfathers and teachers and half-brothers he will be asked to
kill, and in despair he throws his bow to the ground, unwilling to
fight. The man holding the reins is none other than an avatar or
incarnation of God and his teaching about the relative nature of

that moment of despair and inaction makes up the whole of the Gita. It is the same message we find in this logion here—there are times when we must stand up for Reality or Truth, and transcend the ties of family, tribe, church or nation. These are the markers of relative reality and the very things that bar us sometimes from the raw presence and experience we are poised to encounter.

If we look carefully at the voices in our heads that damage us the most, where did they first arise? Often from the mouths of teachers, parents, brothers and sisters, our society, our church, or peers. We are called to be like Mary, Yeshua's mother, when she lifted her eyes up and out of the norms of her social conditioning and said yes to bearing a child, unmarried and alone except for her deep trust in something that transcended the voices of judgment and condemnation within her.

This is deeply troubling for most of us because, like relinquishing our training wheels or choosing a career so very different from what is expected of us, we find ourselves truly alone without the interior or exterior props that we have allowed to guide our lives. We are in a state of pure poverty when we turn away from the dictates of family, tribe, nation and church when they do not align with our own truest voice within. That's a terrifying step to take, but it is the very nature of a faith that can never be taken from us.

Ameyn.

The Eastern Parallels:

"Knowledge of the Divine dissolves all bonds, and gives freedom from every kind of misery including birth and death."

--S'vetasvatara Upanishad

Going Deeper:

Today, simply breathe with one hand on your belly and one on your heart again. If the breath is likened to spirit, what is it teaching you directly today? Write down at least ten words that capture its nature for you, without any expectation of the "rightness" of the words.

Summation:

Trouble arises within us when we realize that our allegiance to family, tribe, church or nation must be secondary to our inner experience of Truth.

Logion 56

Yeshua says,

*"Those who make knowledge
of the cosmos their specialty
have made friends with a corpse,
but the cosmos is not worthy
of those who know it to be so."*

The First Response:
I dubbed him Wilber
and my lab partner smacked me,
sort of playfully on the shoulder—
anything to keep it light enough
so that she wouldn't throw up.
(Nurse wannabes don't all have cast iron stomachs.)
I'd dissected rabbits and chickens and fish for food,
so this bloodless little black and white
fetal pig,
smelly in his preservative juices,
was not so hard to carve, classify and label at all.
It's a mind I enjoy being in—
standing well back and naming, identifying, judging--
except when
the scalpel
is turned
on something still breathing,
when it looks up
and *in*
and for a moment
recognizes that part of me,
of IT and WE
that will never, ever,
be
a corpse.

222

Today in Wisdom's Caravan:

There is always a dance between intuition and our supposedly rational mind. if we spend all our time in Ultimate Reality and learn nothing of the cosmos we will be one-eyed—the trick is the balancing act of the two, honoring both the gift *and* the servant parts of our consciousness. As Albert Einstein once said, "The intuitive mind is a sacred gift and the rational mind is a faithful servant. We have created a society that honors the servant and has forgotten the gift."

To learn the facts of material existence is exciting and necessary in our world, but so, too, these "facts" must be balanced with an understanding of that living spark in the center of everything. Our science still has not been able to fully explain consciousness itself—that alone should make us rather humble when we can't even define the very medium in which all our observations and meaning-making occur.

Trouble for us arises when we take the material cosmos to be the whole picture of reality, one that we can study and know in totality. The person who "knows they do not know" is in a more organic and "free" place than the person who screens reality through just a single lens of academic/scientific study or second hand knowledge. This in no way means that the scientist should be pitted against the spiritual person, but rather, each should use both their intuitive and rational faculties fully in order to be whole.

Ameyn.

The Eastern Parallels:

"Like bubbles in the water, the worlds rise, exist, and dissolve in the Supreme Self, which is the material cause and the prop of everything."

--Shankara

223

"Just as a lamp illumines a jar or pot, so also the *Atman* illumines the mind and sense organs, etc. These material objects by themselves cannot illumine themselves because they are inert."

--Shankara

Going Deeper:

If you were trying to explain this concept of both the rational and intuitive mind functioning together to a young child, what kinds of pictures could you use the capture the idea? Are there any stories you know that point to this balance of rational mind and intuitive sense?

Summation:

Trouble arises within us when we think our relationship with the cosmos is rational, empirical and fully knowable.

Transition Logion 57

Yeshua says,

"God's realm is like this:
A farmer planted good seed
in his field,
but at night, enemies came
and sowed it with weeds.
When he found out,
he did not allow them to be
pulled up, saying,
'No, you might uproot the grain
along with the weeds. Wait till harvest.
It will be perfectly apparent then
which ones are the weeds,
and you may pull them out easily
and burn them.'"

The First Response:

Sometimes the way to work with trouble
is to wait—
no, not in the "count to ten" mode
although, that will keep you breathing--
I mean the kind of waiting that merges with wonder,
that place where we can see our anger
blazing like the sun,
our jealousy like a swamp filled with bird calls,
our injured pride
like the turtle
who lifts his neck long, gazing at the sky.
Trouble can be juicy,
a fresh pomegranate
to be nibbled on until

we can sweep the seeds into the soil,
and trust in things like
ripeness.

Today in Wisdom's Caravan:

The transition logion is delightful today, filled with earthy wisdom about allowing ourselves to put enough space and time around trouble until it begins to shift into something very much like wonder. Emotional states are not stable things, and Yeshua is teaching a kind of deep, agricultural patience and wisdom here. We will know what ideas we have sown into our minds and hearts will bear rich food and what will need to be consigned to the compost pile *if* we give ourselves enough time to live into it all.

The next section coming up is one of *wonder*, although not always the kind that could be labeled as "feel good" energy. Remember, Yeshua is a master storyteller. He'll take us through all the textures of wonder, some of which border on the old meaning of the word "awe" which is a potent mix of energies that include a healthy kind of wide-eyed fearfulness.

But holding both wonder and trouble in the light is a huge part of sovereignty or mastery, words that captures our ability to move with a kind of deep authenticity through our world. That, too, will be part of this Way of Yeshua in its right time.

Ameyn.

The Eastern Parallels:

"There is something good in all seeming failures. You are not to see that now. Time will reveal it. Be patient."

— Sivananda Saraswati

"This world is your best teacher. There is a lesson in everything. There is a lesson in each experience. Learn it and become wise. Every failure is a stepping stone to success. Every difficulty or disappointment is a trial of your faith. Every unpleasant incident or temptation is a test of your inner strength."

— Sivananda Saraswati

Going Deeper:

How do you wait out trouble, until you can clearly see what part of it is weeds and what part is a useable and important lesson? What practices or techniques might keep you engaged in this kind of discernment?

Summation:

Transition: We are filled with wonder when we realize we can put a great deal of space and waiting around times of trouble, and that act will show us both the wheat and weeds of our own minds and hearts.

Trouble arises within us when...

39. we begin to understand that what we thought were our primary sources for searching and finding Truth may have their own agendas and immature understandings, and that we must approach the Truth more intuitively and on our own.

40. communities, thinking they have the "only" view of reality, become cut off from their shared and abundant Source.

41. we are faced with the kenosis that spiritual "finding" demands of us.

42. we realize that to "be" we have to move into the holy present moment, releasing all the burdens of egoic clinging.

43. we do not recognize the "fleshy divinity" of each living thing, including our spiritual masters and furthest stranger.

44. Trouble arises when we name something to come into relationship with it, only to find we find we have tried to concretize infinity.

45. we realize that every thought and action adds to the granary of relationship or isolation, each creating its own fruit in time.

46. we understand we are called to live beyond our spiritual teachers by simply being ourselves and fully conscious.

47. we try to hold two competing spiritual paradigms at once—faith as a culturally conditioned institution or faith as inner experience—and we must choose which path to follow.

48 even as we hold relative and ultimate reality within ourselves, we doubt the inner strength it gives to us.

49. we begin to recognize that the Kingdom is not a realm at all, and that any sense of being "chosen" begs the question: "who is the chooser?"

50. we realize we will only be able to comprehend or verbally express to others what we have "found" in the language of process and paradox.

51. we realize that the new paradigm we are asked to adopt is not what most people expect to find when they begin the spiritual search.

52. we enter into the dualistic mind of comparison in order to create a safe and familiar sense of ground beneath our feet.

53. we think that by engaging in socially mandated rituals, we will deepen our understanding of the Kingdom of Heaven.

54. we face the tension between the very real grace of our "spiritual poverty" and than the false nature of "spiritual materialism".

55. we realize that our allegiance to family, tribe, church or nation must be secondary to our inner experience of Truth.

56. we think our relationship with the cosmos is rational, empirical and fully knowable.

Transition Logion 57: We are filled with wonder when we realize we can put a great deal of space and waiting around times of trouble, and that act will show us both the wheat and weeds of our own minds and hearts.

The Fourth Movement:
The Logia about Wonder

Logion 58

Yeshua says,

"Blessed are the troubled ones.
They have seized
hold of life."

The First Response:

Our insulation plugs in now,
our faces bathed in harsh light
as the evening falls spring-soft,
white petals drifting by,
like static on an old black and white TV.

We do not see it.

Yet, there are still times when
the winds run high,
and the fir trees nod to one another in agreement,
arms spread out wide,
and
one chooses to fall
across the black lines,
sparks flying like the memory
of an ancient storyteller's fire
but blue and silver now,
snapping into the night.

Troubled, our lines of connection
now darkened,
we turn at last to the window
and
behold more than a hundred feet of woody mortality,
belly laughing in the new grass.

Today in Wisdom's Caravan:

We can only be troubled if we unplug enough to pay attention. And yet, here again holy paradox steps in. That moment of turning, of coming into awareness, is also when we blunder fully into wonder and life. As I write this, it is the season of Easter, and that sort of holding life and death, feeling the reality of both deeply, is the very work of this part of the liturgical year and our spiritual journeys.

I am watching wild flowers take over my old manure pile, crows flying haphazardly with brown bits of grass for their nests, sheep freshly shorn in the field, the soft rain of brown dog hair as my pooch frisks by. The Easter story is all around me right now if I choose to see it. There is nothing particularly heroic in it, but the deeper rhythms of life can and do bring tears to my eyes—not out of sorrow, but out of the incredible wonder of all life.

In holding the paradox of death and trouble alongside the riotous joy of living, we come into wholeness as Yeshua wished—each illuminates the other in a kind of brilliance that, once seen, is never forgotten.

Ameyn.

The Eastern Parallels:

"My God is love and sweetly suffers all."

— Śrī Aurobindo

"I swore that I would not suffer from the world's grief and the world's stupidity and cruelty and injustice and I made my heart as hard in endurance as the nether millstone and my mind as a polished surface of steel. I no longer suffered, but enjoyment had passed away from me."

— Śrī Aurobindo

Going Deeper:

Where in life have you experienced this paradox of being troubled and yet filled with life? Recount the story in your journal, both the trouble and blessing held equally.

Summation:

We are filled with Wonder when trouble awakens us into a sense of our wholeness.

Logion 59

Yeshua says,

"Give attention to
the Living Presence
while you are alive
so that when you die and have
the desire to do so
you may have the power to attend."

The First Response:

We are so much more,
than a mosaic,
color tiles of memory,
facts,
plans,
held with running lines of grout.
It's not that we haven't shattered,
cut our fingers on the sharp bits
or tried to glue ourselves together
with water—
but look at the way light plays
with all the colors.
Can you *hear* it?
a child's laughter runs through us like veins,
and out into living gardens and
the slip of a naked body
into cotton sheets
or warm, spring ground.

Today in Wisdom's Caravan:

I am always struck by this logion because it could have
come straight out of the *Bardo Thodol*, better known as the

Tibetan Book of the Dead. Or as one writer translated it, *The Tibetan Book of Living and Dying.* Much of that text is an admonition explicitly and implicitly that we learn to pay attention now so that when we die, we are able to wholly pay attention then as well. This makes of death a wonder, a fascinating movement of life, rather than something to be feared and dreaded.

The year I am writing this, I have been hospitalized eight times and am facing one more surgery. When we simply attend, even our suffering becomes manageable and rooted in a much more spacious reality. Nursing staff and doctors become humanized, food (yes, even hospital food) seems like a feast, and the simple act of walking down a corridor even with an IV pole tagging along is an incredible taste of freedom. Trouble and wonder can dance together if we allow it to happen.

Ameyn.

The Eastern Parallels:

"It is easy to talk on religion, but difficult to practice it."

— Ramakrishna

"If you first fortify yourself with the true knowledge of the Universal Self, and then live in the midst of wealth and worldliness, surely they will in no way affect you."

— Ramakrishna

Going Deeper:

What state of mind do you wish to try to hold as you die? Can you draw it or describe it today?

Summation:

We are filled with Wonder when our daily practice of awareness becomes the way to approach death without fear.

Logion 60

They saw a Samaritan
on his way to Judea,
carrying a lamb.

Yeshua said, "Notice the Samaritan
with the lamb."

His disciples said, "He must be carrying it
in order to kill and eat it."

Yeshua responded, "As long as it is alive he
cannot eat it. Only after he has killed it and it is
dead will it be eaten."

They replied, "What other way is there?"

Yeshua said, "You must be careful
to find a place for yourselves
in the realm of eternal rest,
lest you be killed and eaten, too."

The First Response:

What assumptions do we layer
over all of reality?
Even a scientist will find
his expectations may
influence events
he hoped only to observe.
If I see others only in the
light of utility,
so shall I be seen.

Ask anyone for a dollar,
cold, right on the street,
dressed nicely, hair combed
and
without explanation--
will the person give it to you?
Is it not a wonder?
Your yes or no is
a mirror.

Today in Wisdom's Caravan:

First the disciples notice a lamb, and then Yeshua calls it to their attention again. This is a kind of twin, a double-take, an alert that the teacher is about to point out where two levels of reality are touching in the simple and everyday. Yes, the scene itself is loaded with metaphors for the Middle Eastern mind— the Samaritans who are not part of the Jewish orthodoxy, yet related by both geography and basic beliefs with their Temple-based Jewish neighbors, and the lamb which could be a meal but also a sacrifice or a new addition to a herd.

But the disciples choose to jump to an assumption about the basic needs of the world of relativity—the lamb will be killed so it can be eaten. Yeshua's answer to them seems strange—he points to the lamb's aliveness, and implicitly points out that death narrows all the possibilities inherent in that living presence to a much smaller point. And then he cautions them to find a realm of eternal rest so they themselves won't be eaten.

If his students can rest in the holy present moment, and not jump to conclusions about the world around them, but rather, touch the very aliveness that enfolds them, they will, in turn, not be eaten up by the assumptions that must abound about *them*. For they follow a man without a home, seemingly passive at times, but at others, a teacher who flies in the face of authority and the decorum of their culture. The only way not "be eaten" by a culture that "sees" such things as odd and dangerous is to know, in the way Yeshua knows, that they are alive, vital and resting in the very womb of a larger Reality.

Ameyn.

The Eastern Parallels:

"Clouds come floating into my life, no longer to carry rain or usher storm, but to add color to my sunset sky."

--Rabindranath Tagore

"Do not say, 'It is morning,' and dismiss it with a name of yesterday. See it for the first time as a newborn child that has no name."

-Rabindranath Tagore

Going Deeper:

As you go about your day, choose just one passing person, animal or even tree, and see if you can just meet *that experience* without making assumptions based on your past experiences. What was that moment like?

Summation:

We are filled with Wonder when we realize that when we move in a world without assumptions, we will also find a life-giving place to rest.

Logion 61

Yeshua says,

"Two will be resting on a bed.
One will die,
the other will live."

Salome said,

"Then how is it, sir, that you,
coming from the one Source,
have rested on my couch
and eaten at my table?"

Yeshua said to her,

"I am he who has appeared to you
out of the Realm of Unity,
having been granted that which belongs
to my Father, its Source."

"I will be your student!" she exclaimed.

"Then I say this to you,
if you become whole
you will be full of Light.
If you remain fragmented
darkness will fill you."

The First Response:

Even in the bed of intimacy,
even touching through this thin membrane of skin,
some part of us cries out

we are alone.
We bind to us ideas,
friends,
creative acts,
pets and plants,
careers and homes,
not seeing the armor all things can be.
Come out into the garden tonight,
the moon is just past full,
and if the clouds cover it, no matter.
Sit where you can hear the green exhaling
just for you.
I don't care if you cry the name "Father"
or call to mind the stranger who washed your feet-
vulnerability is not a ritual,
its a fact,
no matter how big the rock we roll before
the cave of our heart.
If you sit with your aloneness
even for the span of ten breaths,
I promise you,
something will stir inside,
and ask
a question—
who is that which thinks
you
are
alone?

Today in Wisdom's Caravan:

The language is intimate—two sharing a bed, and one
will live and one will die. Today I am hearing the echoes of our
deepest aloneness. No matter what we bind ourselves to--
lovers or friends, careers or religions, homes or children--we

242

must at some point face that smallness, that vulnerability we carry within.

Salome, for one moment, heard echoes of the antidote to such a deep wound in the unwavering wisdom of Yeshua. But rather than turn to the experience that would have bound her back with the Source and even intimately with "the Father", she reaches for what is tangible: the human manifestation, the teacher. And Yeshua cautions her, because he could see that movement clearly, from a turning toward the same Light that fills him and then turning away to the outward relationship. He knows, in his aloneness and in hers, he can only point to the Mystery. If his small, alone self is all she clings to, he would be leading her astray. So he tells her, quite bluntly, that if she does not find that union within herself, the "flight of the alone to the Alone" as Plotinus calls it, she will remain fragmented and in darkness. Ironically, once she finds her truest Self, she will be more intimately tied to Yeshua than if she simply tried to cling to the man himself.

Ameyn.

The Eastern Parallels:

"The devotee Uddhava said,
'I cannot bear to be separated from you
And worship your holy feet.
Beloved, I beg you, take me with you
Wherever you are going.'"

Krishna replies:
'Shake off all attachments
Whether to family or friends.
Roam the world as one free of all attachments,
with impartial vision.
To do this,
fix your mind on Me.'"

--The Uddhava Gita

Going Deeper:

The next time you feel very alone, instead of filling that hole with entertainment or "ground" of any kind, allow yourself to just sit with it. Lay aside the journal, turn off the TV and computer, and rest you hands in your lap. Just breathe, focusing on the feeling of that tender, lonely part of yourself. Nothing has to happen; just observe the feeling. And then allow yourself to recognize everyone, billions of us, share this moment with you. What arises from such a recognition?

Summation:

We are filled with Wonder when out of the isolation of our aloneness, we find the intimacy of our Source.

Logion 62

Yeshua says,

*"I disclose my mysteries
to those ready for Mystery—
so keep secret from your left hand
what your right hand is doing."*

The First Response:

I think of dervishes
spinning
one hand up, one down,
around their still point teacher,
and yet
gazing up
all of it sweeping around,
the earth around its sun, the
galaxy around its pivot point,
galaxies upon galaxies spinning
'round the Source.
Left and right,
wrong and right,
all opposites
feather between
gently curved fingers,
the eternal
emptying
fullness
of
Mystery.

Today in Wisdom's Caravan:

When we leave the world of relativity—of dividing the world up into left and right, right and wrong, body and spirit, up and down, we begin to see in a whole different way. Notice that Yeshua cannot give you this non-dual awareness; he can only nudge when you are already primed to experience it, and in that experience, even your distance from your teacher is transcended.

It also gently points to a kind of intuitive mind, the state where you are already single. The experience can't even be "told" from your right to left hand because you have become unified and whole, which is the whole point of "conversion." How do we know without knowing? By *not* using the analytical part of mind that creates division in our conceptions of reality. In a sense, it is to *be* rather than to *do*, to *experience* rather than *analyze*.

Ameyn.

The Eastern Parallels:

"I am not a Hindu, Nor a Muslim am I! I am this body, a play of five elements; a drama of the spirit dancing with joy and sorrow."

"Student, tell me, what is God?
He is the breath inside the breath."

"When the Guest is being searched for,
it is the intensity of the longing for the Guest
that does all the work.
Look at me, and you will see a slave of that intensity."

--Kabir

Going Deeper:

How do we "know" without "knowing"? Walk around with this question for the day, applying it whenever your mind slips into judging, evaluating, etc. At the end of the day, what did you come to "know?"

Summation:

We are filled with Wonder when we come to know the Body that is beyond all opposites.

Logion 63

Yeshua says,

"There was a rich man
who had expendable wealth.
He said to himself,
'I will take my money
and use it to plant, sow, and harvest,
filling my barns with the produce,
then I'll have everything'
--these were the thoughts
occupying his mind.
That night he died.
Listen, if you are paying attention."

The First Response:

If I pour out your life in
a small handful of seeds,
and bid you
drop one a day into the earth,
how would you live differently
from all the days prior?
When that uncountable mound dwindles
and four or five dark specks touch and fold
in the wrinkles of your tightly held fist,
how then?
No, I don't mean you should
do anything different at all
but I wonder,
will you look more carefully
for some small flower you might have started,
uncurling itself like a yoga student
from a forward fold

to stand, arms raised
in the gentle victory
of
just
living?

Today in Wisdom's Caravan:

   Where we place our mind and attention day to day is the same place we dwell. If the Kingdom of Heaven is here and now, if we trust in that basic ground of our being, then we will live an abundant life. If all is placed in the context that everything is always in flux, changing, unpredictable, then the tremendous amount of energy we put into our "future" lives is like casting seeds upon all kinds of unprepared ground. The present moment IS the ground for the future. That does not mean we don't use common sense—storing emergency water and two weeks of canned food in case of an earthquake is perfectly rational here in the Pacific Northwest. Thinking about your pantry and any possible earthquake *all the time* is not. There is a balance to be struck here, the narrow path of being aware of how we use the energy of life given to us.
   This logion also points to the inherent selfishness of many of our thoughts. Who do we plan for? Who do we worry about? Often the subtext is all about ourselves. But Yeshua was trying to raise our eyes a little, to tune into the interrelationship with all life. That small movement of mind broadens into a panorama that cannot help but hold our attention with ease and grace and wonder.
   Ameyn.

The Eastern Parallels:

"Day after day countless people die. Yet they imagine they'll live forever. O Lord, what can be a greater wonder?"

--Yudisthira's Answer, The Mahabharata

"When the Gods deal defeat to a person, they first take his mind away, so that he sees things wrongly. Time does not raise a stick and clobber a man's head; the power of Time is just this upended view of things."

-- Dhritarastra (The Mahabharata: The Book of the Assembly Hall)

Going Deeper:

As you go about your day, gently notice what your mind drifts to most often—planning? worrying? The past? There is nothing you need to do except raise an inner eyebrow and grin.

Noticing *is* the antidote.

Summation:

We are filled with Wonder when we realize how we are able to so easily ignore the inevitability of our death.

Logion 64

Yeshua says,

"A man was throwing a dinner party
and when everything
was prepared, he sent his
servant out to call the guests.

The servant went to the first and said,
'My master invites you.'
But he replied, 'I have set aside some
funds for merchants who are coming this evening
and I will be placing orders.
I beg to be excused from dinner'

So he went to the second and said,
'My master has invited you.'
But he said, 'I have bought a house
which requires a day of my time.
I am too busy to come.'

He went to another and said to him,
'My master invites you now.'
He replied to the servant, 'My friend is
getting married and I am to prepare the
wedding banquet.
I simply cannot come.
I beg to be excused.'

He went to another and said,
'My master calls you.'
In reply he said to the servant,
'I have just bought a farm
and am about to pay taxes.
I cannot come. Please excuse me.

I must be off.'

*The servant returned to his master
and said, 'The ones you invited to the
dinner have all excused themselves.'*

*The master said to the servant, 'Then
go to outsiders and strangers on the
roads. Find folk there and
bring them here to eat.'
Those busy buying and selling
cannot get into my Father's realm."*

The First Response:

The servant said,
"My master invites you.
My master has invited you.
My master invites you *now*.
My master calls you."
Not the public face,
not the market place "you",
not the home owner,
the taxpayer,
the wedding planner—
but rather,
the stranger and outsider
you keep close to your heart
and
who has the ears to heed
and hear.

Today in Wisdom's Caravan:

It might be easy to slip the hook here—be a little smug that you aren't all about business, households, big life rituals and taxes. But then, if we are honest, aren't we all at some level? These are the places where we are most likely to wear our masks, where we can conveniently separate out the sacred from the secular. When we make such a break in ourselves, the part of us that can hear the invitation to come to the lavish table will be cast in the role of the stranger and outsider to our "normal", everyday consciousness.

The wonder of it is that both parts of yourself are being invited to partake in a different way of experiencing the world, all the time, in every moment. This wisdom teacher demands, but gently in the form of invitation and call, that we follow the lead of the intuitive selves, the one's left outside of the "house" of the ego and who wander the roadways in our minds, itinerant as Yeshua himself in his embodied teaching.

We cannot enter into relationship with the other until we enter into relationship with all the parts of ourselves.

Ameyn.

The Eastern Parallels:

"If a person is gifting away his elephant but his heart is set on the rope used for tying the elephant, of what use is his attachment to the rope when he is giving away the elephant itself?"

--Ramayana 2:37:3

"Whatever is one's food, the same food shall be offered to one's gods."

--Ramayana 2:103:30

Going Deeper:

Is there a particular part of your personality that you are more aware of at work? In your home? At social gatherings? What is its purpose and when does it get in the way of listening to your more intuitive self?

Summation:

We are filled with Wonder when we understand that all the parts of ourselves are being gently called to the Communion Table.

Logion 65

Yeshua says,

*"A good and fair-minded man
had a vineyard that he gave
over to tenants to work and make
productive.
When he sent a servant to
collect profit from the vineyard,
the tenants took him and nearly
beat him to death.
When the servant returned he told his
master who said, 'Perhaps they
did not know him.'
So he sent another servant
and they beat him as well.
Then the master said, 'I'll send my son.
Maybe that will shame them.'
But those tenants, because they
knew him to be heir to the vineyard
seized and killed him.
Whoever can hear this, listen!"*

The First Response:

Sight along the line here,
the way the wire and wood
create a cradle for the yellow-green unfurling.
What abundance will sag under the fall sun,
the silver moonlight reflected on
hand-sized leaves
and clusters of purple grapes,
shy,

in their sweet and pregnant roundness.

It's good to remember the way the grain
stood tall, whispered to one another,
before falling in ripe golden tears
and chaff.
Good to feel the yeast and honey and heat
making a new home in sinew
and sharp white teeth.

What does blood wash clean in you?

Do not speak too loudly that you
are the heir to the vineyard,
to the roll of land that is just now
woven and textured in curving rows
unless you can go out,
sleeves rolled up and sweat staining
your sun-burnt arms
and be willing to face
the trampling and scything
care
you must administer
when the sun runs her northern courses
again.

Today in Wisdom's Caravan:

There are many layers here, as in any good parable,
many levels of interpretation, some which seem quite obvious.
But there is a low undercurrent of wonder here, something that
is more than overt resistance and violence. For the truth is
packaged here in our very blood—it is not enough to own the
vineyard and lease it out to others to work and then show a
profit from their labors.

As I've mentioned before, when I come across the image of the vineyard, I almost always connect it to relationship and community—the branches interwoven, the roots laced together beneath the ground, the shared frames holding everyone up, the leveling snip of the pruning shears and the continuance of all our seasons finally mixed in communion wine. A true master will know the way of his plants, the times of waiting and beating sunshine and harvest. Who entrusts such things to tenants who will try to keep the place where they labor and sweat, and who will be resistant to pay the master who is not present and walking with them? These are not the children of an earlier Logion who played in a field not theirs and who stripped naked and stood before the landlords. These will kill the heirs of the vineyard because he asks for coin for what he did not care for, did not trim or sweat for.

The shadow of any kind of spiritual finding is to distance one's self from the *practice* of our faith and our responsibility to others. Our spiritual fields cannot be tended by anyone else, nor can we use proxies to interact with the world. If we are to be masters ourselves, if we are to stand as Yeshua consistently asks of us, we must learn to prune and water and work the soil of our practice ourselves, side by side in relationship with the teachings and other practitioners. Or the offspring of our spiritual work will be killed by those who inhabit the field we own in name alone.

Ameyn.

The Eastern Parallels:

"If you do not pour water on your plant, what will happen? It will slowly wither and die. Our habits will also slowly wither and die away if we do not give them an opportunity to manifest."

— Swami Satchidananda, *The Yoga Sutras*

"Mere philosophy will not satisfy us. We cannot reach the goal by mere words alone. Without practice, nothing can be achieved. "

— Swami Satchidananda, *The Yoga Sutras*

Going Deeper:

In what ways do you "own" your spiritual work and in what ways do you give it over to tenants and expect some kind of payback from them?

Summation:

We are filled with Wonder when we realize that the masterful student must work the field and gather the "profit" not by proxy but by the blisters of his own hands.

Logion 66

Yeshua says,

"Bring me the stone
the builders discarded.
That one will be the key."

The First Response:

The trucks ground them up,
the tractor pushed them aside,
but I?
I went along with my bucket,
picking up the fist-sized stones by hand,
so caked with mud that I had no idea
what they might actually look like.
In my garden, I laid them out,
a rag-tag collection of dirty lumps
scattered amongst
hostas and grasses
and the tender beginnings of
deep green plants from Indonesia.
Now, I watch the skies for rain
curious to see their colors rinsed
fresh and honest
in their apparent uselessness.

Today in Wisdom's Caravan:

Yeshua isn't building walls and churches and fortresses
or even homes. He's looking for the spirit *in* the stone, the way
the light and shadow on its uneven face makes us aware of the
indwelling spirit in everything. Builders see the utility of the

rock. Yeshua sees the beauty, the potential, the mirror and brave one who cannot be framed and stacked and utilized but rather, is able to stand in that incredibly human place of imperfection and the total blessedness of our being.

It's eerie, but I feel like this logion is speaking about the *Gospel of Thomas* itself. If we use a deep and careful reading of this text as the key to unlock the halls of knowledge that the priests and scholars have kept from us, if we use it as the "touchstone" for the New Testament of the Bible, what embedded wonders will open to us?

Ameyn.

The Eastern Parallels:

"Open your eyes of love, and see Him who pervades this world! Consider it well, and know that this is your own country."

-Kabir

"Now I have no caste, no creed,
I am no more what I am!"

-Kabir

Going Deeper:

What parts of you are like a stone that builders have put aside? What might these places tell you about your relationship with God?

Summation:

We are filled with Wonder when we recognize that we stand blessed in all our imperfection that is perfect unto itself.

Logion 67

Yeshua says,

"If you come to know it all,
and yet you yourself are lacking,
you have missed everything."

The First Response:

When books become a conversation for you,
one wholeness listening to another;
when you can watch a horse run
small bucks in a too-tight pasture,
and not evaluate it;
when you can look out over the
low-tide mud-flats
and see how beautifully
the deep brown shines in the sun;
when you understand
the fire and pressure and kneading
the clay of your body has withstood
and find you are not lacking,
then the empty spaces in you
will become useful and
holy.

Today in Wisdom's Caravan:

Our culture is one that values "knowledge" in the form
of facts, figures, information and how information exchanges
work. It's sort of like saying a dollar bill is something important
when really, it is a piece of paper and ink. The value we give it is
from our minds, from crafting ideas about its meaning. We
might command a great deal of philosophical or theological

knowledge, but again, these things are ephemeral and all facts, knowledge and learning can be taken from us.

We are something more than those things.

We gather money, knowledge, facts and ideologies out of a sense of lack. But it is not enough to see the whole world alight and then picture yourself in darkness, as less-than, as anything other than part of an amazing living system. To do so, to make yourself as other than the "good" of creation, is to create separation within yourself and to subtly distance yourself from the blessings of that life.

There is a deeper movement in all things, including ourselves, which cannot be weighed, measured or sometimes even spoken aloud. And unless we touch that wonder, we have missed the essential holiness of everything.

Ameny.

The Eastern Parallels:

"A mind all logic is like a knife all blade. It makes the hand bleed that uses it."

--Rabindranath Tagore

"The water in a vessel is sparkling; the water in the sea is dark. The small truth has words which are clear; the great truth has great silence."

--Rabindrinath Tagore

Going Deeper:

Today, whenever a sense of superiority arises because you think you know something, or if you find yourself born down with a sense of lack of any kind, shut your eyes and breathe into your belly. Reconnect with what is real, what God created and called "good".

Summation:

We are filled with Wonder when we see we don't need to know it all because we are already that ALL.

Logion 68

Yeshua says,

"Blessed are you, who
in the midst of persecution,
when they hate
and pursue you
even to the core of your being,
cannot find "you" anywhere."

The First Response:

In some Buddhist teachings
we're told:
"drive all blames onto yourself."
It's a brilliant strategy, really,
because then you'll come to
understand
that
persecution
comes out of
stiffening
before
another--
denying their words,
decrying their actions,
creating of them an "other"
and
you'll suddenly see
only rigid things *can* contend—
watch the grass and the windstorm
the fish in the current,
the slim slip of green breaking through rock,
water hollowing out canyons.

And then,
the ultimate joke hits--
who is this "self" you're
driving the blame into anyway?
(Yes, you certainly can smile now
or say
amen .)

Today in Wisdom's Caravan:

I like this logion very much for its practicality. Yeshua is not saying that we will not face persecution in all its many shades and flavors, but rather, if you are resting in that spaciousness of ultimate reality, there is no "you" there to injure. It's a natural and lovely concept—when the ego or the dualistic "you" stiffens against something, there can be injury. But when "you" are soft, pliable, less invested in your egoic self—in other words, when you are more deeply associated with your true Self—there is "no one" there to harm.

Such wisdom abounds in nature, as a few lines of the poem above point out. Truth is like that—mirrored so clearly in the play of natural world around us. The trick is to take the teachings in and make them a reality for our nimble and contentious minds.

Ameyn.

The Eastern Parallels:

"As large as this ether (all space) is, so large is that ether within the heart. Both heaven and earth are contained within it, both fire and air, both sun and moon, both lightning and stars; and whatever there is of him (the Self) here in the world, and whatever is not (i. e. whatever has been or will be), all that is contained within it."

--Chandogya Upanishad

"Arjuna, the ideas of heat and cold, pleasure and pain are produced by the contacts of the senses with their objects. Such ideas are limited by a beginning and an end. They are transitory, O Arjuna; bear them with patience!"

--The Bhagavad-Gita 11:14

Going Deeper:

Recall for yourself a time when you stiffened against a perceived insult. Now, imagine how the insult feels when you are "larger" and grounded in a more spacious reality. How might you remember to do this in day to day life? Is there a touchstone (quite literally) you can carry in your pocket, a rock or piece of sea glass for instance, that when you finger it, can remind you of your larger ground and process?

Summation:

We are filled with Wonder when we find there is no hard and fast "me" within us who really can be persecuted.

Logion 69

Yeshua says,

"Blessed are all those
who are persecuted right into
the depths of their own hearts.
Only there will they come to know
their true Father and Source.
Blessed are all the hungry ones.
Their inner longings will be satisfied."

The First Response:

I tried, really tried,
to shut up and watch,
to let them find out if love and transcendence
could really anchor their tent.
The wind was blowing hard,
and I watched how they struggled with that—
the canvas snapping,
the clouds boiling, tumbling
lifting the walls
with fingers of rain and hail.
Their hands shook as they pounded,
looking for firm ground beneath
the mud.

Better to just let the thing fall,
and trust that
when it hangs up on some snatching tree branch,
there will be shelter there enough.

Enough.

I remember what you said to Mary—

"Don't cling to me..."
Not much bread and wine there
to chew on, to swallow.
It's a chancy thing, God—
to use suffering as a window.

Today in Wisdom's Caravan:

Anytime Yeshua gives a teaching twice in a row, watch carefully. Notice how he is leading us to the idea that suffering of any kind *can* be like a kind of useful hunger because our emotional "why me?" opens the door by tearing down all the ways we armor ourselves against the world. In that hunger, in that questioning heart thrown wide open, we can at last begin to glimpse the depth and strength upon which our seemingly fragile lives are really built.

When that cry comes out of the deepest part of our heart, we end up face to face with our Father and Source, the very ground of our being. This is not a path that denies the very real physical and mental aspects of suffering, but rather uses that energy in a transformational way to create union and relationship by fueling a more authentic search.

Ameyn.

The Eastern Parallels:

"The fire that warms us can also consume us; it is not the fault of the fire."

— Swami Vivekananda

"Comfort is no test of truth. Truth is often far from being comfortable."

— Swami Vivekananda

Going Deeper:

Can you name a great suffering or sorrow or hunger that opened your heart to a sense of the spirit around and within you? Or was it many small pecks from the world that contributed to how you view Mystery now?

Summation:

We are filled with Wonder when we come to see that our deepest reaction to persecution and suffering creates the very questions that open our heart.

Logion 70

Yeshua says,

"When you give birth
to that which is
within yourself,
what you bring forth will save you.
If you possess nothing within,
that absence will destroy you."

The First Response:

Have I looked into Your face,
and not seen a thousand-thousand ripples
of creative outpouring?
Forgive me then,
I did not understand.
Words and walls You've
pushed aside now,
and in the place where
I once imagined a labyrinth laid out
in stone and shell,
the sheep are grazing, knee-deep in greenest grass,
their winter coats dirty
but their ears flicking,
as they walk, spiraling.

Today in Wisdom's Caravan:

Echoing the previous two Logion, this capstone captures
the essence of Yeshua's teaching on how to work with
persecution and suffering—by birthing (making manifest) the
firm conviction that relative reality is not all there is. It is one

270

thing to understand that deep suffering can be a window into the divine, quite another to live out of that knowledge.

This logion can also refer to any movement within that is life affirming—an authentic response to our world that arises out of our more experiential connection to our Source. Giving birth is not an act of will so much as the inexorable force of things ripening and moving toward wholeness. But in order to be birthed, there must be something there that is tangible, that is a potent mix of you and the Truth you have wed. There must have first been that silent and wordless Yes. And out of that Yes, we birth our own salvation.

Ameyn.

The Eastern Parallels:

"O friend! hope for Him whilst you live, know whilst you live, understand whilst you live: for in life deliverance abides.
If your bonds be not broken whilst living, what hope of deliverance in death?
It is but an empty dream, that the soul shall have union with Him because it has passed from the body:
If He is found now, He is found then,
If not, we do but go to dwell in the City of Death.
If you have union now, you shall have it hereafter."

--Kabir

"If you don't break your ropes while you're alive, do you think ghosts will do it after?"

— Kabir

Going Deeper:

What does *birth* mean to you in all its realities and metaphors? Write about the many textures this word can display and then look at this logion again. How is this multivalent word a clue to fully living in spiritual wonder?

Summation:

We are filled with Wonder when we comprehend that in deeply affirming our great Yes to Mystery, we will, from our relationship with That, birth our own salvation.

Logion 71

Yeshua says,

"I will destroy this house
and no one will ever
be able to rebuild it."

The First Response:

Peek-a-boo
in sea-glass and seaweed,
in dark chocolate and raspberries,
in this brush of hand past hand,
in the silent house, moonlight streaming in,
in an old dog's eyes
and the empty sanctuary,
flowers fading on a driftwood cross.
I will chase You,
laughing,
beyond the sagging rafters of tradition
and the flaking cement of dogma and creed.
Things do fall apart,
at least the stuff of
beginnings
and
endings.

Today in Wisdom's Caravan:

How we construct it, this cage we call an ego, and think it house and home! How we preserve it, with the cement of the past and the shadowy hopes of the future. How we armor it,

273

with many locks of self-righteousness, of ideologies and dogmas and handed-down belief. What poor hosts we can be to what is not family or tribe, to what is uncomfortable or new to us. I can go on, but you see the powerful analogy that Yeshua (and the Buddha) make here: The house we think we have in our precious egos are not our True homes.

They are prisons.

And when we come to see that, when we break what is rigid and guarded and even comfortable and secure, we finally begin to understand what Yeshua means by the son of man having no place to lay his head (Luke 9:58). Neither do we, if we want to follow this Way in all honesty and courage. We instead will be at home in the universe, a placement of heart that can never be taken from us.

Ameyn.

The Eastern Parallels:

"Oh housebuilder! You have now been caught!
You shall not build a house again.
Your rafters have been broken. Your ridgepole demolished.
The nirvana has been attained.
And every kind of craving has been uprooted and destroyed."

--*Dhammapāda*, verses 153,154 (Buddha speaking to the Lord of Illusion)

Going Deeper:

What image or piece of music captures for you what it would feel like to live a life that is not bound by the walls and roof of your expectations, beliefs, affiliations and self-consciousness?

Summation:

We are filled with Wonder when we realize that we do not need to be prisoners in the house of our egos.

Logion 72

A man said to Yeshua,

"Speak to my brothers
so that they will divide
my father's belongings
with me."

Yeshua replied to him,
"Sir, who has made me the divider?"

He turned to his students and asked
"Am I here to divide?"

The First Response:

They picked up garbage along the beach,
cool 14 year old boys,
but I watched their eyes,
constantly lifting,
the way they held their bags,
let the wind catch and fill them
like ship sails.
Later, they plunged,
Amazonian,
into gullies and blackberry-tangles
gloved hands reaching for that
plastic bottle just out of each.
I hunted along,
pointing out this red straw,
that bit of Styrofoam,
but the boys?

They had the better part.

Today in Wisdom's Caravan:

Where do we place most of our attention, day in and day out? The great gift of meditation is to show us precisely where—the past and future, or sometimes if we are too focused, we're driven by the work of the moment, narrowed, and consumed. I'm not talking about the kind of creative or artist or athletic focus which is embodied being working on all its cylinders, but rather, the way we can divide ourselves throughout the day.

This passage is so poignant when we look at the very real fact of religion against religion, national against nation, neighbor against neighbor, and at all the parts of ourselves at war. Once we understand that unitive consciousness is real, then we realize that there can be no *ultimate division* at any level of the many systems of our world. You cannot say "yes" to God and continue to invest in the divisions because that is a symptom of forgetting, unripeness or what we sometimes call sin.

Ameyn.

The Eastern Parallels:

"When you win and the other fellow loses, what do you see? A losing face. There is great joy in losing and making the other person win and have a happy face. Who will be the happiest person? The one who brings happiness to others."

— Swami Satchidananda

"Devotion gradually progresses to higher levels. . . . One type goes to God and asks Him to remove his suffering. Another one will ask for money or material things. A third will request liberation or release from his bondage. And the fourth will not ask for anything. He will just enjoy praying and praising his Lord. That is the highest form of prayer."

— Swami Satchidananda

Going Deeper:

As you sit, gently close your eyes and inhale the many textures of the inner world—your fears, your memories, your plans, all of it. Then exhale out a sense of floating in the center of everything, upheld and unified. Continue for as long as you like, then finish with an "amen."

Summation:

We are filled with Wonder when we see that we cannot believe in the oneness of God and continue to divide and evaluate the world, thinking that is the only or greatest level of reality.

Logion 73

Yeshua says,

"The harvest is abundant.
The reapers are few.
Implore the Master of the Harvest
to send out workers."

The First Response:

I'm afraid to say abundance
because it will be misunderstood.
Folks will run out and buy wood
to create grain storage barns,
or toss out their old clothes
and gas up for a shopping trip.
Look, that fellow is even digging
a new wine cellar,
not even noticing where he is
flinging the dirt.

I really mean to say that starlight just kissed
the white Rhodie bloom
and even in the grayness,
I can see it blushing.

Today in Wisdom's Caravan:

The wonder is that the harvest is so very rich, and stands
there naked all the time for us to come and claim it. Again, I
hear so clearly that Yeshua alone is not the reaper, that all of us
are called to stand, harvest, and pass on, our eyes fixed on that
Unity that has created such a lavish display of wealth.

Abundance is so often misused in our spiritual lingo. The truth is, we always have abundance if we just choose to see. And the only place we can see this is when we are present, when we show up and harvest the veritable feast for all of our senses and empty inner places. That is the central prayer here, to awaken through grace and practice into that consciousness that will infuse such a gift into the very marrow of our existence.

Ameyn.

The Eastern Parallels:

"The Lord is One, but He is diffused in many forms. Bring in, bring in, that All-pervading Lord."

--Sant Ravidas

"The house is large, its kitchen vast,
but after only a moment's passed,
it's vacant..."

--Sant Ravidas

Going Deeper:

On days that you feel small and huddled, take the time to see the abundance that infuses your world. Can you make a list...sunshine on a green wooden fence, birdsong, the way traffic can express a time of waiting and receiving, the ferry's departing whistle like a call to awaken? Once you begin to see it here and there, with practice and grace, you will see it everywhere, the abundance that can never be stolen, that will never rot away.

Summation:

We are filled with Wonder when we grasp that abundance is always at hand, in a form that never can be taken from us and will never die.

Logion 74

Yeshua says,

"O Lord,
many have gathered
around the fountain,
but there is nothing in the well."

The First Response:

There have been times
when I have sat in my car after a church service,
watching the folks walk away,
hands in pockets,
heads tipped to cell phones.
I have wandered back into the sanctuary
after all had left,
stood there, silently waiting,
(like I did as a child,
for that one, high-pitched note
inside the ear of the ear of the ear)
trying so hard to carry
water droplets
from a dry fountain.
It takes a while to let the music fade,
to recall
how the flute player settled his instrument
with such loving care,
to stop rolling words over in my mind,
and remember how
the associate priest's voice trembled
and his hands shook on Palm Sunday--
so much more honest than a professional cantor,
and the silence that rimmed him 'round

told me about loving God,
like a sip of
fresh
clear
water
at last.

Today in Wisdom's Caravan:

After the wonder of abundance, these cautionary words stand stark and clear as a hand-clap at night. I recall the woman at the well, the repartee she and Yeshua shared as they dipped for water that would never run dry and would ease the deepest thirst. But now, as in Yeshua's day, we look for that living water in the wrong places: following the crowd, making dogmas and creeds into inflexible laws, turning to the self-help books and Youtube.com personalities that flare up like brief fountains. We try to understand why we still thirst without diving deep within and finding out why nothing fills our buckets and the holes in our hearts.

Here again is an invitation, this time cast in the *negativa* shade—where is your Source, the place within that runs brimming with cold, clear water? Are you willing to dig for it, search for it, stand alone for it? The promise between this logion and the one previous is the same. You *will* find, as all the logion 1-19 promised. And your thirst will be slaked. And that promise is a wonder to our souls.

Ameyn.

The Eastern Parallels:

"Whenever we cling to anything that is continually changing, we will become more and more insecure with the passage of time."

--Eknath Easwaran

"When we start to suffer, it tells us something very valuable. It means that we are not seeing the truth, and we are not relating from the truth. It's a beautiful pointer. It never fails."

--Adyashanti

Going Deeper:

How do you show up at your well—your book club, your church or temple, your job? What do you need to do to find water there instead of looking at a fountain that seems to have gone dry?

Summation:

We are filled with Wonder when we realize that both our sense of abundance and our sense of thirst arrive from the same place in our hearts, each balancing the other in holy paradox.

Logion 75

Yeshua says,

"Many are standing
at the door,
but only the single
or solitary will enter the place of union."

The First Response:

One by one.
That's mostly how doors are made to go through.
Daily we practice it,
grimace or laugh
(depending on our day)
when shoved up against the frame by another.
Even the bride must gather her skirts,
as the onlookers clap and snap photos with their iPhones,
cling tightly to her groom
as he sweeps her beneath the lintel.
They know the precious secret-
just like Mary did--
not one, not two.

Today in Wisdom's Caravan:

We do not pass through any physical doorway as a
crowd. And those rare moments when we step through a door
with another, we're united whether our minds like it or not—
squeezed and mushed together or carried like a bride. Mostly,
we have to step through alone, our shoulders squared and our
eyes wide open in authenticity.

One by one we make our passages, from birth to death, the many doors of glass and wood and accomplishment and embarrassment swinging open and then shut. And we do it alone, at least to those watching. It doesn't mean there isn't a crowd of friends on the other side. It doesn't mean that the whole group gathered won't sift through, slowly, like dust on sunbeams. They will. Or they won't. That's not our work or our practice.

Yeshua came to open doors, to fill fountains, to harvest the field, but his call to each of us is unique. And that is the wonder.

Ameyn.

The Eastern Parallels:

"You can't cross the sea merely by standing and staring at the water."

— Rabindranath Tagore

"If I can't make it through one door, I'll go through another door- or I'll make a door. Something terrific will come no matter how dark the present."

— Rabindranath Tagore

Going Deeper:

What doors have you recently journeyed through? Can you draw or name them? Who waited on each side as you left and as you entered?

Summation:

We are filled with Wonder when we receive the message that all our inner fountains will be filled, the doors open, the harvest waiting only for our single and eternal Yes.

Transition Logion 76

Yeshua says,

*"The Father's Realm
can be compared to
a merchant who discovered
a pearl hidden in a consignment
of goods. Wisely he returned the goods
and bought the single pearl himself instead.*

*You too must seek out
for yourselves an enduring treasure
in that realm where moths
cannot get in to eat
or insects come to destroy."*

The First Response:

It's a simple rhythm-
be disturbed or attracted,
then
take the time to be aware of
what nature,
and traffic snarls
and snores
feel like in the body.
Or how thought can snare both your ears
and twist them around your nose,
rodeo style.
We always have the mic before us,
always glasses
always hearing aids,
but do we use them?
Do we want to?

Walk this uphill path with me,
past the small ferns uncurling
through the body of the deadfall,
through the scattered Trillium,
their edges pinkening
before they rest for another year.
Watch your step here,
the water rushing over green stones,
the subtle flash of scales in the shade.
No, it's OK to whistle your way along,
the birds will stare at you,
and share the tune with their flock
at night.

Today in Wisdom's Caravan:

Much knowledge, like consignment merchandise, passes through our hands. It belonged to another, we might have made a little mental income from it, but we did not find it ourselves nor does it move us in any way. It's just business, just entertainment. But every now and again, a pearl glows in what we're reading, listening to, absorbing from teachers. Unlike simply moving the knowledge through our hands, this is the kind of knowing we take home and keep close to our hearts. There pearls grow even more luminous worn close.

It is a wonder to find such a pearl of wisdom, and when we take responsibility for aligning our life with what we have found, we enter into the phase of the spiritual journey we call "reigning" or "sovereignty". This is not the very public kind of Caesar energy, but rather more like Lao Tzu's ideal ruler who "the people do not even know is there at all." It is also like St. Francis' admonition to his fellow monks—"Preach the Gospel always, and sometimes, use words."

The sayings that follow will look deeply at what it is to actively live out of the knowledge of unity consciousness, Christ consciousness, and the dance of relative and ultimate reality.

Ameyn.

The Eastern Parallels:

"There's no value in digging shallow wells in a hundred places. Decide on one place and dig deep. Even if you encounter a rock, use dynamite and keep going down. If you leave that to dig another well, all the first effort is wasted and there is no proof you won't hit rock again."

— Swami Satchidananda

"The moment you understand yourself as the true Self, you find such peace and bliss that the impressions of the petty enjoyments you experienced before become as ordinary specks of light in front of the brilliant sun."

— Swami Satchidananda

Going Deeper:

It is useful to sketch or write out what you think reigning means to you right now. Say a little about what a sovereign soul might be like in the world. Then watch as the next section unfolds and compare what you have drawn or written to the teachings of the wisdom master Yeshua.

Summation:

We are filled with Wonder when we know that we have found the "pearl of great price", bought it, and begin to reign out of it.

We are filled with Wonder when...

58. *trouble awakens us into a sense of our wholeness.*

59. *our daily practice of awareness becomes the way to approach death without fear.*

60. *we realize that when we move in a world without assumptions, we will also find a life-giving place to rest.*

61. *out of the isolation of our aloneness, we find the intimacy of our Source.*

62. *we come to know the Body that is beyond all opposites.*

63. *we realize how we are able to so easily ignore the inevitability of our physical death.*

64. *we understand that all the parts of ourselves are being gently called to the Communion Table.*

65. *we realize that the masterful student must work the field and gather the "profit" not by proxy but by the blisters of his own hands.*

66. *we recognize that we stand blessed in all our imperfection that is perfect unto itself.*

67. *we see we don't need to know it all because we are already that ALL.*

68. *we find there is no hard and fast "me" within us who really can be persecuted.*

69. *we come to see that our deepest reaction to persecution and hunger creates the very questions that open our heart.*

70. we comprehend that in deeply affirming our great Yes to Mystery, we will, from our relationship with That, birth our own salvation.

71. we realize that we do not need to be prisoners in the house of our egos.

72. we see that we cannot believe in the oneness of God and continue to divide and evaluate the world, thinking that is the greatest level of reality.

73. we grasp that abundance is always at hand, in a form that never can be taken from us and will never die.

74. we realize that both our sense of abundance and our sense of spiritual thirst arrive from the same place in our hearts, each balancing the other in holy paradox.

75. we receive the message that all our inner fountains will be filled, the doors open, the harvest waiting only for our single and eternal Yes.

    Transition Logion 76: We are filled with Wonder when we know that we have found the "pearl of great price," bought it, and begin to reign out of it.

The Fifth Movement:
The Logia about Reigning

Logion 77

Yeshua says,

"I am the light
shining upon all things.
I am in the sum of everything,
for everything has come forth from me,
and towards me everything unfolds.
Split a piece of wood,
and there I am.
Pick up a stone
and you will find me there."

The First Response:

If God is in stone,
and tree
and the long, thin finger of the English Ivy,
why take so long
haggle so hard,
about what words mean?
Love is sprinkled liberally
falling everywhere,
and any explanation is simply
God explaining God to God.
Once you get there,
that place where,
fish-like,
you swim in God,
you will walk out
in sweatshirt and jeans
arrayed like a king or queen.

Today in Wisdom's Caravan:

How we reign depends on how we first comprehend life itself. If everything is liberally and equally leavened with God, including ourselves, then reigning is not "over" anything. Rather, it is walking with the calm awareness of our belonging, our truest identity, our "enough-ness". If we think we are separate, needy, poverty-stricken, we will react in ways that will attempt to acquire, or ward off what others could take from us. We reduce ourselves to our skin, our possessions, our ideologies.

Reigning or moving through the world with a sense of sovereignty, is a kind of inner dignity that is unaffected by things like apparent change, status, gender, money, and all the other ways we try to fill the sacred hole in our heart. But God is already home, deep within us, and as we truly awaken to THAT, we walk not just in abundance but in grace. It is our inner touchstone, and looking outward, we see it reflected over and over again in community and harmony.

Ameyn.

The Eastern Parallels:

"The plums tasted
sweet to the unlettered desert-tribe girl-
but what manners! To chew into each!
She was ungainly, low-caste, ill mannered and dirty,
but the god took the fruit she'd been sucking.
Why? She knew how to love."

--Mirabai

"Beauty is truth's smile when she beholds her own face in a perfect mirror."

--Rabindranath Tagore

Going Deeper:

Today, as you move through the day, practice sensing God in the world. Do you notice that you cannot acknowledge that divinity unless you are present and aware? What does that say to you about the very nature of God?

Summation:

We reign in our lives when we sense the heart of Mystery in all things,
universally.

Logion 78

Yeshua says,

"Why did you come out
into the wilderness?
To see a reed
blown about by the wind?
A man dressed in soft raiment
like your rulers and the powerful?
Yes, indeed, they are clothed in fine
luxurious garments,
but what they lack
is the ability to discern truth."

The First Response:

Sorry.
The clothes do not make the man,
nor is standing stiff before everything
the mark of a wild one.
In nature, even the predators are fluid,
grace-filled;
they know their purpose and reason for being.
Truth requires a softer, sidelong eye,
like taking off your glasses in the blazing sun,
and seeing the soft shadows of shapes
backlit and alone.
There, you might be able to read a truth
that media did not program into your vision
nor expectations cloud.
Our work then, is to learn to do this
in the dark
and fearlessly.

Today in Wisdom's Caravan:

Reigning requires a way of looking beyond the stories told by fine trappings or titles, a way of seeing that holds both the relative and ultimate realities in gentle but fearless hands. We must use a kind of inner flexibility, a sense of our own and others true proportions, that are not anything other than dry grass and eternity knit together.

I can hear Yeshua's deep sigh here, even though there is no leading question to trigger this saying. He knows he is no more lasting than a reed in the wind, nor does he parade in soft clothing. He is neither John, the wild ascetic man, nor a priest. He is simply ourselves mirrored back to us, awakened, without a mask or persona to go before him.

Ameyn.

The Eastern Parallels:

"What is seen is not the Truth
What *is* cannot be said
Trust comes not without seeing
Nor understanding without words
The wise comprehends with knowledge
To the ignorant it is but a wonder
Some worship the formless God
Some worship his various forms
In what way He is beyond these attributes
Only the Knower knows
That music cannot be written
How can then there be the notes
Says Kabir, awareness alone will overcome illusion."

— Kabir

Going Deeper:

Over 80 percent of our language is actually non-verbal, so clothing, movements, and expressions are as vital as words. Add to that the idea that we tend to see what we expect to see (why magic works so well), and it's sometimes very difficult to get to the core of what is actually being communicated. Today, try to see through the layers of social conditioning by simply meeting each person's eyes and become wholly present to them, beyond clothing, titles or names. How does this feel?

Summation:

We reign when we stand unified in the face of truth, vulnerable and without any props.

Logion 79

A woman in the crowd said to him,

"Fortunate is the womb
which bore you,
and the breasts
which nourished you."

Yeshua turned to her and said,

"The ones who hear
the Father's Word
and guard its truth
are truly fortunate.
But the days are coming
when you will say,
'Lucky is the womb that never bore,
and the breasts that never gave milk.'"

The First Response:

Lift your eyes now,
the volcano floats in a cloak of red,
and all the clouds whisper fire
one to another.
Even in the cool evening,
pressure and heat rage beneath my feet
and over my head.
Maybe that is why I like living here
where the stony ground can move at any time
or a tsunami lap voraciously at the edges of all we have built.
Truth is paradoxical at its core,
and yet
the beauty
endures.

Today in Wisdom's Caravan:

As in the Synoptic Gospels, this message is hard to hear at first—the overtones of gloom and doom tend to stop up our more sensitive "intuitive" ears. And yet, hope brings us back to the text, to listen deeper. When we reign, we will be accorded accolades—remember when Buddha was asked if he were an angel or a god? And he replied, "no, I am merely Awake." This is what Yeshua is hinting at here—if you believe your parents were blessed to have had you, if you believe the hype around you, then surely you will face the opposite and be brought low.

Hear, also, *how* he gently deflects the compliment. Yeshua knows that his energy and glow come from his oneness with God, and that is the blessing he focuses on. It is not that he is denigrating the flesh here, but rather, his words point to the deep gnosis that enlivens not just his life, but the lives of all.

Ameyn.

The Eastern Parallels:

"People see his pleasure ground; Him no one sees at all."

--Brihadaranyaka Upanishad

"But the wise, self-controlled, and tranquil souls, who are contented in spirit, and who practice austerity and meditation in solitude and silence, are freed from all impurity, and attain by the path of liberation the immortal, the truly existing, the changeless Self."

--Mundaka Upanishad

Going Deeper:

Today, think back to a time of either great praise or blame, and then connect with your sense of union with God. Once you are grounded, feel how you might respond out of that place of reigning, that state of mind that sees truth and speaks/acts out of compassion. What would you have done or said differently as you faced the energy of others?

Summation:

We reign when we are able to remain grounded in that union with God, even in the face of compliments and curses alike.

Logion 80

Yeshua says,

"Whoever knows the cosmos
discovers the body,
but the cosmos
does not deserve the one
who makes that discovery."

The First Response:

How could you look through a telescope
and not sigh with wonder,
sighting back along the twist of our DNA,
the very dust of sperm and egg,
blazing against the night.
Holding your hand now before your face,
curl your fingers around eternity,
seeing your own body arrayed within like the galaxy,
the electrical arcs of the mind
the Milky Way,
and yet
and yet
when you raise your eyes to the Beloved,
matter falls away,
or rather,
plunges into
the creative dynamic of the
spaciousness
unending
now.

Today in Wisdom's Caravan:

Once we become aware of our body (like our clothes, or status) we are called to look even deeper. It's the question of "who am I?" brought to the foreground, and when we search into that with clarity and fearlessness, we can only come to the answer of Tat Tvam Asi or Thou are THAT. As amazing as our body is, it is always in flux, our thoughts like lightning, ephemeral and then lost in spaciousness. Yet, we find in that ever-changing cosmos within and without a still point of being that was never born and never dies. This focus opens for us a way to stand in change, *be* change, and yet reign with wisdom and compassion.

Again, the body is not so much denied as exposed for the ever changing material and mental construct that it is. Without compassion, we might disdain it and the cosmos. But with our hearts grounded in Love, indeed knowing we *are* the Beloved in a real sense, we find the balance point where wisdom and compassion inform and support each other. We see our fleeting physical existence, even as we reach out to sustain and nurture everything around us. In that place, we find both the human and the divine, and unified, we see with eyes of Christ.

Ameyn.

The Eastern Parallels:

"The meeting of man **and God** must always mean a penetration and entry of the divine into the human and a self-immergence of man in the Divinity."

--Aurobindo

"What men call knowledge, is the reasoned acceptance of false appearances. Wisdom looks behind the veil and sees."

--Aurobindo

Going Deeper:

Look deeply into a mirror, seeing the passage of years. And yet, as you look, can you also see in yourself a continuing, abiding Presence that unifies the past with the future in the NOW? Which is more real for you? What might you do, in the unique expression of your life, to express that Presence in your everyday life?

Summation:

We reign when we unify the wisdom of seeing our infinity with the compassion of holding our finiteness in the present moment.

Logion 81

Yeshua says,

"Let whoever becomes rich
be king,
but let whoever holds power,
surrender it."

The First Response:

What does it take to reign in
your life, your world?
Can you float when given both the smile and frown,
open your hand to endless wealth,
no matter what your bank account claims,
and stay grounded
when faced with joy or despair around you?

No, you don't need to be a saint,
or forget to feel—
indeed,
that might be the very crux of that
slippery
word
called
sin--
but rather
place everything in its context,
not with just your agile mind,
but in the deepest resounding cave of your heart.

Today in Wisdom's Caravan:

What is the difference between reigning and power? between wealth and riches? Yeshua's secret is simple—if you can release power, your clinging to wealth, your personal sense of control and or shadowy attempts at perfection, then and only then are you fit to reign. Being a temporal king is not the same thing as what he is trying to convey. He's looking for something deeper than the masks that we place before our true faces and hearts, those things that attempt to take the place of a more lasting energy and abundance.

Notice he is not saying you cannot have fine things, or be seated in positions of power; rather, he is saying don't let such things rule *you*. That is real reigning, seated in the place where we have choice to let go or utilize the gifts of being embodied in a way filled with both wisdom and love. In that space, we are in deep relationship with not just God but those around us, and all because we are full and complete in ourselves.

Ameyn.

The Eastern Parallels:

"Seek ye first the kingdom of God, and everything shall be added unto you." This is the one great duty, this is renunciation. Live for an ideal, and leave no place in the mind for anything else. Let us put forth all our energies to acquire that which never fails--our spiritual perfection. If we have true yearning for realization, we must struggle, and through struggle growth will come. We shall make mistakes, but they may be angels unawares."

--Swami Vivekananda

"All that is real in me is God; all that is real in God is I. The gulf between God and human beings is thus bridged. Thus we find how, by knowing God, we find the kingdom of heaven within us."

--Swami Vivekananda

Going Deeper:

In what way are you ruled by the material wealth of your life (or lack thereof)? How might you begin to practice the divine equanimity that Yeshua is teaching in your own life?

Summation:

We reign when we are conscious that the difference between temporal kingship and reigning hinges on our ability to release control of outer circumstances, even as we are grounded in the abundance of our union with God.

Logion 82

Yeshua says,

**"Whoever comes
close to me
dwells near fire.
Whoever moves away from me
remains far from the kingdom."**

The First Response:

Even wrapped in my winter blanket,
I can feel it,
the way the sun slants now,
brilliant,
through my makeshift curtain of prayer shawls.
My small black dog stretches in that
warm luxury,
the light catching its share of gray and browns
in her painfully shining fur.
When she notices my stare,
she yawns and in her mouth
the universe unfolds,
endless fires
waiting to cook me
until I am
completely
un-done.

Today in Wisdom's Caravan:

The positive associations with fire—the teaching circle in
which we gather, the light, the warmth, the ability to transform

hard vegetable and meat into sustenance for our bodies—these are the gifts that Yeshua hints at. It is a much more dynamic version of the communion table, the fire of transformation unveiled and spoken out clearly.

And those who cannot face that light, that heat, that transformation? They will be far from the experience of heaven all around and within us. Because Yeshua realizes that for some, changing the way they see and understand reality feels like they themselves are being burned away, feels like the food has become charcoal, that the light is so blinding that their eyes water and they turn away. At the deepest level, the fire followed him to the cross when he cried "Father, why have you forsaken me?" and then finally and forever cooked him into the perfect heart that went far beyond the "me" of that single, poignant cry.

Ameyn.

The Eastern Parallels:

"If there is anything besides the Self there is reason to fear. Who sees the second? First, the ego arises and sees objects as external. If the ego does not rise, the Self alone exists and there is no second [and hence, no fear]."

--Ramana Maharshi

"Remain still, with the conviction that the Self shines as everything yet nothing, within, without, and everywhere."

--Ramana Maharshi

Going Deeper:

In what way do you avoid the "cooking" of being near your best image and lens of the divine? What does that feel like when you are far way in your actions and thoughts from the divine Mystery?

Summation:

We reign when we fully surrender to the light, heat, and transformation that is the heart of the spiritual journey.

Logion 83

Yeshua says,

*"Images are revealed
to humanity while the
light within them is hidden
by the brilliance of
the Father's light.
It is God who is being revealed,
but the image of God
remains concealed
by the blaze of light."*

The First Response:

Are we not a dance of image and icon?
Like naming and thinking we know,
like holding a solid fact and
believing we understand the dynamic
gray ever-becoming motion
within the black and white,
we are shot through with images of God!
But until they burn,
until we have touched the ash with our damp
fingertips,
rubbed and seen
how we can wear a cross on our forehead for a time
then wash it away
but never be free of it,
we will
not understand
how to see within each seed,
each mirror,
each pair of eyes searching our own,

and find
the eternal
Icon.

Today in Wisdom's Caravan:

In every major religion of the world, we are told that we cannot see God. That our limited nature will not allow us to hold everything that God is, and so we perceive it as light, as the full, blazing creative energy that reveals as much as it conceals.

Statues, stained glass windows, and texts all offer us a particular glimpse at God, and all limit God at the same time. We need our objectifications when we begin our relationship with the Mystery. But there will come a time when we must understand them for what they are—so many lenses and no one of them capturing the full extent of God.

As we come into reigning out of that understanding, we begin to see ourselves, too, as valid expressions of the Living One, fully empowered and asked to enter into compassionate relationship with all of life. We then become a light, a way for others to begin to turn toward God and see through our lives the creative outpouring of our Source.

Ameyn.

The Eastern Parallels:

"By whatever means I must get the direction realization of the Lord. The religion of today consists in repeating the name of God every now and then, in praying to Him in the presence of everybody and in showing people how religious one is; I do not want it. If the Divine is there, there must be a way of experiencing His existence, of realizing His presence; however hard the path, I have taken a firm resolution to follow it..."

--Aurobindo

"Hard it is to be in the world, free, yet living the life of ordinary men; but because it is hard, therefore it must be attempted and accomplished."

--Aurobindo

Going Deeper:

What image of God do you hold dear? Are you able to perceive not just it but also yourself as a lens through which the light of God can shine? Why or why not? What ramifications does this have for your life? For the lives of others?

Summation:

We reign when we understand that we blaze with the light of God and become an avenue for that wisdom and compassion to enter into relationship with creation.

Logion 84

Yeshua says

"When you see your own projection
into time and space
it makes you happy.
But when the time comes
that you are able to look
upon the icon of your own being,
which came into existence
at the beginning,
and neither dies
nor has yet been fully revealed,
will you be able to stand it?"

The First Response:

The first time it happened,
it was an Australian summertime.
That night,
on the beach, we walked for a time,
children from all over the world,
and wondered at the bits of life
that glowed in the dark.
We threw the sleeping bags out on the red earth,
just on a rise above the sea,
and watched the Southern Cross roll itself against
the backdrop of an ocean
of glitter,
the ether so alive
it seemed to undulate like black moss.

And I, early in those cold morning hours,
understood an ancient way of time

317

when everything stopped,
when everything went still,
but the stars bent their light around the earth,
no more timeless than I
no more finite than I.

Today in Wisdom's Caravan:

Our egos are very frightened when they come to see
that they are a construct of conditioning, experiences, roles and
habits. Those first few glimpses of ourselves as something
larger, timeless, and networked into everything can be terrifying
even as they are also full of ecstasy. The trick is to live the day-
to-day routine, to stop at the red light, to cook dinner, and do
the laundry even as each object, each moment, each breath is
also deeply sacred. It's a way of life that honors both our
ephemeral natures and our deeper continuous being in God.

We are ever unfolding, moving like the galaxies that spin
out from some still point, the microcosm to the macrocosm. In
that sense, change is the very ground of our being, and paradox
cannot be avoided because we encompass all opposites, like
being the energetic signature of both in-breath and out-breath.
All that wisdom way of seeing can be frightening without the
corrective that Yeshua gives us: a deep relational compassion
that tells us we are never alone in this and can never fall out of
God, as a minister friend of mine likes to say.

Ameyn.

The Eastern Parallels:

"I seem to have loved you in numberless forms, numberless
times, in life after life, in age after age forever."

— Rabindranath Tagore

"The small wisdom is like water in a glass:
clear, transparent, pure.
The great wisdom is like the water in the sea:
dark, mysterious, impenetrable."

— Rabindranath Tagore

Going Deeper:

How do you practice holding both your sense of timelessness and the passage of time? Can you capture this realization in art, music, or words? How does compassion feel when added to this gnosis?

Summation:

We reign when we are able to release the ego and rest in its timeless becoming, tempered with compassion.

Logion 85

Yeshua says,

"Adam came into being
out of a great power
and fullness,
and yet he is not superior to you.
Had he been prepared for it,
he would not have tasted death."

The First Response:

My cousin made etchings of
headstone knights in England,
the overly tall and slender stone carvings
caught on black paper
and gold crayon,
rolled and tubed and carried by air to this mythical land,
America, then
framed to stare out over televisions
and lounging poodles
and pizza boxes.
Some folks wear a bracelet of tiny skulls,
others like to wander through old cemeteries,
or old family albums.
We sip death,
no more than two fingers at a time,
like testing for an allergy,
like trying on a too-sexy dress
on a rainy and cold afternoon.
Maybe that is good—
just enough flavoring to make us
awaken.

Today in Wisdom's Caravan:

It is not enough to be created in the image of God. Even Adam, directly formed and breathed into life by the Mystery did not manifest the consciousness that allows us all to go beyond the duality of life and death. That was the corrective that Yeshua was trying to instill in us, rather than the shadowy sense of original sin which didn't even become a clear doctrine in the church for centuries.

The taste of death is not the experience of actual death, but rather, the worry, the anxiety, the shadowy presence of our mortality that tints and flavors everything we do. It is the unconscious "elephant in the room" that we spend so much time running around. Our birthright is to see death fully and say "yes" to this manifest fact of life, even as we understand our "yes" is also a complete belief that this caravan we walk with will go forward joyfully.

Ameyn.

The Eastern Parallels:

"Death is as sure for that which is born, as birth is for that which is dead. Therefore grieve not for what is inevitable."

--The Bhagavad-Gita

"Governing sense, mind and intellect, intent on liberation, free from desire, fear and anger, the sage is forever free."

--The Bhagavad-Gita

Going Deeper:

What is your favorite way to avoid the truth of your physical death? In what ways do you look it boldly in the eye in your day to day life?

Summation:

We reign when we understand that we have the capacity to overcome our fear of death and live with joy and enthusiasm.

Logion 86

Yeshua says,

"Foxes have dens
and birds have nests,
but the son of humanity
has no place to lay his head and rest."

The First Response:

Would you know rest?
Come here and sit beside me on the front porch.
The sun has warmed the cedar boards,
and picked up the greens and browns of the grain
like a piece of fine art.
Look here,
study this free-form cement pad,
and see
how seeds from the birdfeeder
have fallen into the cracks and
beautiful weeds are unwinding from this
strange new soil.
The slug line glistens,
the seemingly dead pinecones roll under
the nervous sole of your tennis shoe.
Even in this snapshot,
everything is in motion
eternally.
Rest is
knowing
that you
really can
float
on

this
river of
change.

Today in Wisdom's Caravan:

While we move through this life, fully embodied, rest is a relative thing, like seasons, like breathing. We are in motion always. Even when asleep our body is repairing, assimilating, the work of being alive going on even when we are not at all conscious of it.

If a true rest awaits us, it is in learning to float on that current of motion, neither attached nor shoving its truth away from us. In a sense, Yeshua is saying that reigning is not about getting ground under our feet, or setting up a palace of the mind where things are unchanging and secure. Rather, he is asking us to see that our personal sovereignty depends upon our ability to be comfortable with the ambiguity and activity that is the very nature of life. That is the greater rest.

Ameyn.

The Eastern Parallels:

"God laughs again when two brothers divide their land with a string, saying to each other, "This side is mine and that side is yours." He laughs and says to Himself, "The whole universe belongs to Me, but they say they own this portion or that portion."

--Ramakrishna

"Live in the world like a waterfowl. The water clings to the bird, but the bird shakes it off. Live in the world like a mudfish. The fish lives in the mud, but its skin is always bright and shiny."

--Ramakrishna

Going Deeper:

How do you work with the energies of fatigue, ambiguity, and constant change in your own life? Name some of the concrete tools you use, or use the time to research a technique or way you'd like to learn more about.

Summation:

We reign when we understand the deepest nature of mastery is actually learning to relax into ever-present energy of change that is the reality of relative existence.

Logion 87

Yeshua says,

"Miserable is the body
that depends upon a body,
and the soul
that depends upon both."

The First Response:

I AM
birdsong sprinkled on gravel road
road bending into the valley,
valley filled with skunk cabbage
cabbage floating in ginger sauce
sauce and mango swallowed into body
body flopping on the bed in sunshine
sunshine colliding with dust motes
motes in my sister's or brother's eye
eye to see it all
all, in its wholeness
and holiness
AM I.

Today in Wisdom's Caravan:

This has been my lesson in this difficult year of hospital stays and surgeries and illnesses. The body cannot be depended upon to be unchanging. Like the wisdom of India chortles, "it is a wonder that each day we watch the funeral procession go by us and think we shall never die" (*The Mahabharata*). And indeed, it is worse for a soul who mistakes its clarity and

326

timelessness with the body, and evaluates itself on that ever-sliding scale. Are you lessened as a human being when you cannot "produce" or "look good"? What is the soul's answer?

It is important to understand that the body is not denigrated here, a common mistake of our own dualistic Christian heritage. Rather, Yeshua is asking us to again hold the relative and the ultimate faces of reality and not confuse the two ways of being in the world. Pick up any book of art from the ages and what is considered "beautiful" will vary enormously from century to century. So, too, what thoughts are considered "holy", "scientific" and "factual" will shift in time. The soul must become the still point that holds ultimate reality and gives the deeper meaning to our being embodied, thought-filled creatures.

Ameyn.

The Eastern Parallels:

"[O]ur own bodies are changing every second. Yet we take the body to be our Self; and, speaking in terms of it, we say, "I am hungry" or "I am lame"; "I am black" or "I am white." These are all just the conditions of the body. We touch the truth when we say, "My body aches," implying the body belongs to us and that therefore *we* are not that."

— Swami Satchidananda

"However strong or beautiful this body may be, its culmination is in those three pounds of (cremation) ashes. And still people are so attached to it. Glory be to God."

--Sri Sharada Devi

Going Deeper:

How has your body either elevated or let you down over the years? What has been the effect of that elevation or let down on your soul? Is the perception of this pitching ship of your body changing as you age?

Summation:

We reign when we place our seat of wisdom in the soul of ultimate reality without denigrating the vehicle of our bodies so firmly situated in relative reality.

Logion 88

Yeshua says,

"The angels and the prophets
will come and bring you
what already belongs to you,
and you will give them
what you have to give.
But ask yourself this:
when may they come
and receive back from you
what already belongs to them?"

The First Response:

What is the exchange rate for a
prophetic voice in the wages
of our age?
How do we value the angel,
the miracle,
or
the times when we stood in all
our glorious aloneness
and
could
do
nothing?
The very cloth on your body is
woven of under and over threads,
cotton relationship caught up
in nap and hue,
and tell me
where does the prophet or angel
end
and you

begin?
When you can effortlessly name that weave,
in your own word and metaphors,
then,
with grace,
will you reign.

Today in Wisdom's Caravan:

As you are probably picking up if you have read this far, it would be natural to write a commentary on this Gospel that totally focused on relationship—not just the relationship between human and human, but the trembling web of existence, where everything is in relationship with everything else. This is not just a world of economies and exchanges, of lenders and borrowers, of businesses and workers, of armies and commanders, but rather, the kind of relationship that exists between your in-breath and out-breath, between the day and night, between the moment just before creation and that continued outflow.

It is an intimate thing, this relationship that Yeshua points to. I refer to it as a kind of Yoga in the title of my book because that is what Yoga *is*, a Union, a yoking together of energy and matter that is the very cresting and ever-moving wave of creation. When Yeshua spoke out of his own understanding of such a dance , he used the word Abba, Daddy, to describe his dance-partner. His actions showed how he was immersed in that deep relationship, well beyond the reach of words. Here, in this logion, he calls us to consider our utter inability to stand "alone"—not because we are weak or out of inflated pride, *but because that is not our reality*! Notice, this does not mean we are not to *stand*, a word he uses frequently to mean our ability to discern our needy grasping at false support and our ability to step clear of such things. The paradox is, in our standing, we come to see that we are never alone, interwoven as we are with all that is. Ameyn.

The Eastern Parallels:

"If we only look within, we will see the Light as if we were seeing our own image in a mirror. (122)"

— Swami Satchidananda

"Doesn't the Bible say 'blessed are the pure in the heart, so they shall see God?' when? Only when there is purity in the heart; a heart peaceful and free from egoism--the 'I'and the 'mine.' Purity of heart and equanimity of mind are the very essence of Yoga."

— Swami Satchidananda

Going Deeper:

What metaphors would you use to capture the difference between relational power in this world and how Yeshua is trying to convey it? What pictures might capture this for you?

Summation:

We reign when we stand up firmly in the relational I AM, discerning accurately the shared and interwoven life that is THE power of God.

Logion 89

Yeshua says,

"For what reason would you
only wash the outside of a cup?
Do you not realize
that the creator of the outside
is the one that made the inside was well?"

The First Response:

Iced tea,
hot chocolate,
Dr. Pepper,
Spanish Mocha,
orange juice,
water of course,
lots of that.
I've swirled them around in my
black bear
tribal cup,
enjoying
the crisp white totem symbol
that flares out even
when I need a sip at midnight.
Her wise, slanted eyes and flattened nose
tell me the truth, though-
the most useful thing about a cup
is
its perfectly accepting
emptiness.

Today in Wisdom's Caravan:

The inner is as equally created by God as the outer—the inner that allows, discerns, opens, accepts, builds relationship, fosters creative outflow, and holds memory. That is the place and state where past, present and future meet in constant dynamic chaos, undershot with a deep river of silence. Much of the Gospel of Thomas reflects this movement of the awareness and care of inner selves, particularly this ephemeral thing that we call our consciousness in all its hues and textures, even as it gently shows us how much time we actually put into caring for the ultimately unreal masks, the form, the persona—in other words, the outside of the cup.

Reigning is about learning the language of the empty chalice—being able to use its poetic words like allowing, accepting, holding or containing, structuring and nurturing in a way that frames our relationships and makes them the very stuff of holiness.

Ameyn.

The Eastern Parallels:

"When the scriptural philosopher dissects words and thoughts with the scalpel of his reason, he may grow so fond of theoretical knowledge and of mentally separating wisdom into various segments that he may "dry up" through lack of the experience of truth in divine ecstasy. If a person spent his lifetime in analyzing the properties of water and in examining water from different sources all over the world, he would not thereby quench his thirst. A thirsty man, without fussing over the atomic constituencies, selects some good water; drinking it, he becomes satisfied. An exoteric jnana yogi—a follower of the path of discriminative reason—may read and analyze all the scriptures and still not slake his soul thirst."

--Yogananda

"God is the life behind your life, the sight behind your eyes, the taste behind your tongue, and the love behind your love. To realize this to the fullest extent is Self-realization. Without God's power you can do nothing."

--Yogananda

Going Deeper:

Create for yourself a list of the attributes of the empty cup. What do your words tell you about reigning?

Summation:

**We reign when we embody the qualities of the empty cup,
clean within and without,
so that we might be of the most transparent use.**

Logion 90

Yeshua says,

"Come to me
for justice is my yoke,
and gentleness is my rule,
and you will discover the state of rest."

The First Response:

I shade in pictures of
shattered pottery
rearranged in line drawings
and 0.33 mm coloring sticks—
a memory of a thing's memory—
broken to give me
a little piece of calming monotony
that also shimmers
and seems for a time
beautiful.
How simple it really is,
to see how God ripples salmon-like
through the opaque waters soaking us,
and know
I really only have to raise my eyes
from my ordered marker palette
to touch gentleness,
to touch rest.

Today in Wisdom's Caravan:

There is no strain in the way of Yeshua. Restlessness,
strain, willfulness—these things are the wages of maintaining

335

our personas and masks, instead of working easily in the harness, the yoke, with the God who suffuses everything. Justice arises simply out of rightly seeing reality for what it is, as does gentleness and rest. This deep authenticity is the very ground, not only of reigning without effort, but also manifesting the deep relationship we have with all of creation.

The act of yoking (*union, yoga*) is the act of being in compassionate connectivity with the wholeness of life. Because nothing is outside of that yoke, the "work" of living becomes simple. We no longer need to prove ourselves, fight for or against anything because when anything is viewed through this holy lens, everything becomes doable—a working with, rather than against. This is the very harnessing of wisdom with compassion that frames much of Buddhist thought as well.

Ameyn.

The Eastern Parallels:

"Give up this dry discussion, this hodge-podge of philosophy. Who has been able to know God by reasoning? Even sages like Suka and Vyasa are at best like big ants trying to carry away a few grains of sugar from a large heap."

--Sri Sarada Devi

"Even the impossible becomes possible through devotion."

--Sri Sarada Devi

"What else does one obtain by realization of God? Does one grow two horns? No, the mind becomes pure, and through a pure mind one attains knowledge and awakening."

--Sri Sarada Devi

Going Deeper:

When you think of the word "justice", what images or impressions or words arise for you. Did you link gentleness and rest with this word as this logion does? Why or why not?

Summation:

We reign when we understand that the "work" of justice, gentleness, and rest becomes effortless when we are yoked with the wisdom and compassion of God.

Logion 91

They say to him,

*"Tell us who you
really are, so we
may believe in you."*

*He said to them,
"You have learned to read
the face of earth and sky,
but you do not yet recognize
the one standing in your presence,
nor can you make sense of
the present moment."*

The First Response:

How do you control the present moment?
By laying over it
an expectation—
call it a bias—
that folds the senses like a baby blanket.
The predictability is comforting.
If I told you
the person you see day after day
is never the same,
the road you walked before lunch,
the soup you lift on the battered silver spoon,
is always
shivering and shifting,
some part of you might not sleep.

You will listen too deeply to the night.

Today in Wisdom's Caravan:

Yeshua captures here an important element of our daily consciousness, what we might call an overlay of expectation. That's what belief does—creates a script that effectively frames the way we interact with reality. His disciples want him to author it for them, the way he should be seen and addressed and understood.

But one of the most important reasons Yeshua taught at all was to call attention to this energy of belief, particularly as it masks the present moment and our ability to see into reality. Belief allows the manipulation of people, of nations. Belief is almost always verbal, a layer between what is actually felt or experienced and what is expected. As long as we lean on belief, we will never be free.

Understand that I am not talking about faith, which is experiential, pre-verbal, whole-body and cannot be taken from you or bent to another's use by ill-meaning professional religious or political entities. The truth Yeshua is showing us is how little *faith* we actually have, and how difficult it is to come by when blocked by our "usual" way of mentally operating in the world. If we would "see" our teacher and call him by name, we can only do that in the unguarded and spacious present moment. And once seen there, it will be evident everywhere and always.

Ameyn.

The Eastern Parallels:

"In a conflict between the heart and the brain, follow your heart. "

— Swami Vivekananda

"Dare to be free, dare to go as far as your thought leads, and dare to carry that out in your life."

— Swami Vivekananda

Going Deeper:

Read a piece of poetry to yourself. Take a few moments of silence, and then read it out-loud. Did anything change in that experience for you? Sometimes, when reading out loud, we don't have our "blinders" on quite so tightly, and new meaning and tones will creep into the experience. In what other ways could you interact with reality so that you are wholly and completely present?

Summation:

We reign when we come into the present moment without the bias of belief or the comfortable constructs that keep ground beneath our feet.

Logion 92

Yeshua says,

"Seek now, I say,
and you will find
that for which you search.
You see, I am ready to tell you
everything you were asking earlier
and did not explain
but at the moment
no one is searching out anything."

The First Response:

Can you look this way?
Even for a moment?
Do I have to climb onto this cross
again,
so
you will see?
Even that event,
echoing in artistic media through ages,
is a mumble if
you do not once raise your eyes
to Mine.
Mary learned more from a single
aborted
touch
in the garden
than you do,
so bowed over that scripture,
so inclined to that sermon.
You drop your head at the proper times,

fingers flicking over the imagined cross of your chest,
but when I scream across the ages,
"Look at Me! HEAR ME!"
how quickly your hand reaches for the i-phone--
Just so *you* can feel.
Just so you don't have to *feel*.

I cannot turn My face from you,
and you, circles of your mind already widening
with the daily,
nudge Me away
like foam
riding on salt water.

Today in Wisdom's Caravan:

This is one of the "poignant" logion for me, the sad and
resigned sigh of Yeshua who knows that when we begin to reign
out of our sips of gnosis, one of the dangers of this stage of the
spiritual journey is that we will think we have wholly arrived.
We can become jaded even with knowing, making it stale and
automatic and in that moment, we have lost what we tried so
very hard to find and make our own. I can imagine him,
standing ready to answer questions that never come. Questions
arise out of the beginner's mind, the fresh mind. At this
moment in time, he is aware how alone he is, in the silence
around him as his disciples retreat into comfortable numbness.

As a Christian culture, we often miss the deep aloneness
that Yeshua experienced. That may be the second teaching
here—that we will not be well seen, well understood, as we
stand up into this gift of awakened consciousness And that
aloneness will be deeply painful at times—not so much *for*
ourselves, but out of compassion for those sleepwalking around
us. It does not mean we slide into spiritual pride, nor cut off our
relationship with others, only that our responsibility is vast

when we take up this work. And we will feel it, deep in our bones, as we reign.

    Ameyn.

The Eastern Parallels:

"If you want the truth, I'll tell you the truth:
Listen to the secret sound,
the real sound,
which is inside you."

— Kabir

"Do not keep the slanderer away,
treat him with affection and honor:
Body and soul, he scours all clean,
babbling about this and that."

— Kabir

Going Deeper:

How do you plan to keep your spiritual life fresh? What small steps would awaken you to "hear" and "question" and "see" the world in all its textures as Yeshua wishes for us?

Summation:

We reign when we do not fall back to sleep in the midst of our life, thinking that having seen once, we will always see or having heard once, we will always hear.

Logion 93

Yeshua says,

**"Do not give what is sacred
to dogs who will only
discard it on a manure pile.
Do not cast pearls in front of pigs
who will only trample and ruin them."**

The First Response:

I.
Unclean,
both the dog and swine to
the people of Yeshua's place
and time—
or that is what their professional religious
tried to tell them.
My lab looks up at me,
her great pink tongue thrusts out
in a wide grin
and I smile back.
To my eye,
sacred pearls
are no more or less than this—
my hand gliding over her soft ears,
the way she puts her paw on my knee
and looks deeply at me.
Sometimes, I notice people have trouble meeting my eye,
but she?
She studies me a moment,
then runs to fetch a ball.

II.
I know nothing about pigs,
though I showed them once,
at a little county fair
framing the stout arch of their backs with the cane,
like weighing dew-dripped hills
on a desert's flat scale.
Their eyes are small, squinting, but
intelligent,
and my father feared for me
when I stepped into that pen.
Competitive omnivores,
pig and I,
and he knew my show clothes
would not protect me.

III.
Perhaps the injunction isn't about the spiritual readiness at all—
The layman, canny, resourceful,
kind, sensitive,
knows
it is the human being,
the professional,
mantled and powerful,
who will try
to wring sustenance and love
from abstractions and clammy excretions.

Today in Wisdom's Caravan:

I know there is a "pat" way of interpreting this particular logion. It appears in the Synoptics (Matthew 7:6) and most of us who have graced pews in our lives have heard over and over about spiritual readiness. But I scratch my head when I find it here, settled amongst the "reigning" logia, a pearl and a bit of wisdom cast before us.

For Yeshua, everyone was potentially *ready*, inherently able to hear, deeply unified within even though sleepwalking, and he is usually quite free using nature, animals, indeed rocks and chopped wood to reveal the sacred. So what is it besides "unreadiness" that keeps us from hearing? That is the more interesting question to me. The injunction against "unclean" practices, "unclean" animals, are all based in the purity codes of the religion of his day. Those who would see such animals as unclean would be the professional religious, and we have heard many times the ways that Yeshua warns us against outer piety and outer cleanliness. Perhaps, then, he is warning us not to try to instruct the professional religious, those who will not understand what treasures they have been given because they are operating out of a wholly different sense of what constitutes reality and exhibit the deepest kind of uncleanliness: ignorance.

I don't mean to target *all* religious professionals; here, in this context, we're looking at the priests of the Temple who may have been not only colluding with Rome to keep their own people captive, but who were also deeply invested in the status and wealth of their powerful positions. To try to instruct them would have been foolish and dangerous, something that Yeshua himelf learned first hand. Those who reign should follow the good counsel of St. Benedict's Rule: "Offer advice only when asked and then with great reluctance."

Ameyn.

The Eastern Parallels:

"Most people believe the mind to be a mirror, more or less accurately reflecting the world outside them, not realizing on the contrary that the mind is itself the principal element of creation."

— Rabindranath Tagore

"By plucking her petals you do not gather the beauty of the flower."

— Rabindranath Tagore

Going Deeper:

Can you recall a time when you offered spiritual insight that was not asked of you? How did that feel to you, both emotionally and intellectually? What was its outcome?

Summation:

We reign when we offer spiritual advice only with great reluctance and only when asked.

Logion 94

Yeshua says,

"Those seeking will find
what they are looking for.
Doors will swing open
for the ones who knock."

The First Response:

If you open a book of poetry
in a language you cannot read,
what value does it have?
I will tell you this—
let a native reader flow the words over you,
and watch their eyes, moving,
the way their skin flushes,
the twitch in their fingers
or when they must turn aside,
sipping water.
You may not ever intuit the content in full,
but you will remember how to
feel.

Today in Wisdom's Caravan:

Following hard on the heels of Logion 93, Yeshua then
seems to reassure his disciples that the doors of the Temple,
now seeming shut to them, will be open within, and that the
spiritual hunger that drives us all consciously and unconsciously
will be assuaged. In other places he has said that the
professional religious hold the keys to the halls of knowledge,

but they do not enter in. Now he tells us that we have only to knock or ask in full honesty and appreciation and that knowledge will be made available to us.

It is not outside in, but rather, gnosis arising from the inside in the first place. The great Persian poet, Rumi, makes a similar statement when he says he knocked and knocked at wisdom's door only to find he was knocking from the inside. That is the place of reigning, the vantage point of the throne of the heart within ourselves.

Ameyn.

The Eastern Parallels

"Look at you, you madman! Screaming you are thirsty and dying in a desert when all around you there is nothing but water!"

--Kabir

"Do not go to the garden of flowers!
O friend, go not there;
In your body is the garden of flowers.
Take your seat on the thousand petals of the
lotus and there gaze on the infinite beauty."

--Kabir

Going Deeper:

How do you knock inside, at the door of your own wisdom and heart? What techniques work to throw open that portal? Attention, music, conversation, art, silence?

Summation:

We reign when we are willing to believe that all must knock on wisdom's door from within, and it will always be answered.

Transition Logion 95

Yeshua says,

"If you have money,
do not lend it at interest.
Give it instead
to those from whom you
cannot take it back."

The First Response:

The best spiritual advice is like
listening to a street musician play,
his head bent over his guitar,
the crowds eddying around him,
and then,
it happens--
the silence folds around just his notes,
everything slowing down,
the strings vibrating,
the hand drifting back and away,
and he lifts his eyes
to meet your own.

Today in Wisdom's Caravan:

The theme of how to handle spiritual knowledge with
wisdom and compassion continues in this transition logion.
Spiritual knowledge is not like displayed goods in a market
place, nor like money lending where you expect to get back
more than what you gave. Remember, if our model is to be
open, unfilled spaciousness, getting back is *not* the currency of

awakening--it is the way of economics and building up of the self.

Besides teaching us how best to reign within such knowledge, this is also the first intimation of resting—no withdrawal from society, no creating spiritual commerce with it either. This is what it means to be restful, giving what we can, not looking or figuring the return for our efforts. Like taking away a filter before a candle, we are able to blaze and light the rooms we enter effortlessly. That is the secret of restful reigning—activity without grasping after fruits.

Amen.

The Eastern Parallels:

"We have a right to our actions but not the fruits of our actions."

--The Bhagavad-Gita

Going Deeper:

Is there something in your life that you give away without any hope or wish of a return? If not, try to be generous with something material, giving it without any attachment or even hope of a thank-you. How did that feel? How do you do this with thoughts and ideas?

Summation:

Transition: We reign when we can give of our spiritual understanding freely and without expectation of any kind of return for this will bring us our greatest peace and rest within.

We reign when:

77. we sense the heart of Mystery in all things, universally

78. we stand unified in the face of truth, vulnerable and without any props.

79. we are able to remain grounded in that union with God, even in the face of compliments and curses alike.

80. we unify the wisdom of seeing our infinity with the compassion of holding our finiteness in the present moment.

81. we are conscious that the difference between temporal kingship and reigning hinges on our ability to release control of outer circumstances, even as we are grounded in the abundance of our union with God.

82. we fully surrender to the light, heat, and transformation that is the heart of the spiritual journey.

83. we understand that we blaze with the light of God and become an avenue for that wisdom and compassion to enter into relationship with creation.

84. we are able to release the ego and rest in timeless becoming, tempered with compassion.

85. we understand that we have the capacity to overcome our fear of death and live with joy and enthusiasm.

86. when we understand the deepest nature of mastery is actually learning to relax into ever-present energy of change that is the reality of relative existence.

87. *we place our seat of wisdom in the soul of ultimate reality without denigrating the vehicle of our bodies so firmly situated in relative reality.*

88. *we stand up firmly in the relational I AM, accurately discerning the shared and interwoven life that is THE power of God.*

89. *we embody the qualities of the empty cup, clean within and without,*
so that we might be of the most transparent use.

90. *we understand that the "work" of justice, gentleness, and rest becomes effortless when we are yoked with the wisdom and compassion of God.*

91. *we come into the present moment without the bias of belief or the comfortable constructs that keep ground beneath our feet.*

92. *we do not fall back to sleep in the midst of our life, thinking that having seen once, we will always see or having heard once, we will always hear.*

93. *we offer spiritual advice only with great reluctance and only when asked.*

94. *we are willing to believe that all must knock on wisdom's door from within and it will always be answered.*

Transition Logion 95: we can give of our spiritual understanding freely and without expectation of any kind of return for this will bring us our greatest peace and rest within.

The Sixth Movement:
The Logia about Rest

Logion 96

Yeshua says,

*"The Father's realm
can be compared
to a woman
who takes a tiny bit of yeast,
folds it into dough
and makes great loaves
out of it.
Whoever has ears for this, listen!"*

The First Response:

How do you yeast your day?
With the gentle touch,
the joke at the right time,
the tissue handed over without comment or advice,
filling the bird feeder,
scratching the dog ear,
putting aside the novel to greet the person at the door
without any resentment or echo of characters
in your eyes.
It's more than being present.
It's the motion of engagement,
the relationship movements,
folding grace into
the bread of our lives.

Today in Wisdom's Caravan:

We fold the yeast of our spiritual selves into our day by remaining engaged, present, simple and giving. In truth, the

Spirit is blended into us as salt in water, as yeast well-kneaded into bread. When we live out of the knowledge of this, we feed not just ourselves but those around us, coming to the very heart of this teaching, which is the art of graceful and conscious relationship with everything. This is the rest that Yeshua is trying to convey. It is not about withdrawal, not about taking the higher rung on hierarchies of wealth, status, or even spiritual prowess. It is life well lived at the zero sum, a place where there is no effort in our lives because the vast amount of energy we usually expend shoring up our egos and furthering our own agendas falls away. But life itself does not fall! It enriches us even more, adding energy to energy.

Ameyn.

The Eastern Parallels:

"Place this salt in water, and then wait on me in the morning." The son did as he was commanded.

The father said to him: "Bring me the salt, which you placed in the water last night."

The son having looked for it, found it not, for, of course, it was melted.

The father said: "Taste it from the surface of the water. How is it?"

The son replied: "It is salt."

"Taste it from the middle. How is it?"

The son replied: "It is salt."

"Taste it from the bottom. How is it?"

The son replied: "It is salt."
The father said: "Throw it away and then wait. . .on me.

He did so, but the salt exists forever.

Then the father said: "Here also, in this body, . . . you do not
perceive the True, my son; but there indeed it is.

"That which is the subtle essence, in it all that exists has its self.
It is the True. It is the Self, and you, Svetaketu, are it."

--Chandogya Upanishad

Going Deeper:

How do you yeast your day? What practices help you be
present and engaged with the world?

Summation:

**We enter into rest when we yeast our lives with simplicity,
honest relationship, and a sense of transparency.**

Logion 97

Yeshua says,

"The Father's realm
is like a woman carrying
a jar full of meal.
While she is walking on a path
some distance from her home,
the handle on her jug breaks,
and the meal spills out
behind her on the road.
She is unaware of the problem,
for she has noticed nothing.
When she opens the door
of her house
and puts the jar down,
suddenly she discovers it empty."

The First Response:

Our burdens can trail out behind us,
while we, unaware,
trudge our long way home.
Something breaks, something leaks,
but
heaviness has its ways of lifting
and who knows
perhaps manna in the wilderness
was
someone's darkness released
to sky and cloud
transformed
to fall
as food for others.

Today in Wisdom's Caravan:

Resting for Yeshua is about choice—how we respond to the accidents, the meaness, the joys and the friendships of our lives. He does not teach about a God who has taken free will and is capricious; rather, he teaches that while anything can happen, how we respond to those events is wholly in our hands. If we can maintain the mind of reigning, then we will find even the most difficult situations of our lives are actually rest-filled.

Resting does not mean inaction, it means attentive and engaged action. The woman goes out, and purchases meal to make into bread. (*Bread*, in Aramaic, also hints at the energy of life.) Her energy trails out behind her and when she has returned home, to her center and place of attention, she finds she is empty. The two handles she has, wisdom and compassion, have been split—the wisdom or compassion of her full awareness has broken. But when she is whole and ready and can see with gentle eyes what her lack of attention has cost, and bless what has been spilled out as food for the birds, the insects and the ground, she moves again to unification. When her wisdom and compassion are reunited, she'll be able to fill the emptiness of the jug again, bringing food and life back within her.

Ameyn.

The Eastern Parallels:

"We are not going to change the whole world, but we can change ourselves and feel free as birds. We can be serene even in the midst of calamities and, by our serenity, make others more tranquil. Serenity is contagious. If we smile at someone, he or she will smile back. And a smile costs nothing. We should plague everyone with joy. If we are to die in a minute, why not die happily, laughing?"

— Swami Satchidananda

"Happiness is not be sought outside. It can never come from outside or from inside--because it simply is. It is always. Where? Everywhere."

— Swami Satchidananda

Going Deeper:

How do you fill your jar? How do you react when you find it empty? Are there actions that allow you both recognize the emptiness and fill that space out of an attitude of rest?

Summation:

We enter into rest when we move in the world of actions with both wisdom and compassion.

Logion 98

Yeshua says,

"The Father's realm
is like a man wanting
to kill someone powerful.
So he draws a sword
in his own house
and puts it through the wall
to test whether or not
his hand is actually strong enough.
Then he goes out and slays the giant."

The First Response:

How tired they seem,
a surging mania,
their social action signs waving,
their breath like so much mist
dissipating on the air,
their fingers gripping their convictions
like plants in loose soil.
The firs lean close,
ever polite,
and the water laps not far away,
its rhythm set by the lamp-light moon.
All things must act,
even God
but
what heavenly bodies
nudge those demonstrators,
and Who do they see
when the soldiers
come

to the fence line?

The owl hoots one last greeting
from the deep
and closes his golden eyes.

Today in Wisdom's Caravan:

"All things must act," it says in the Bhagavad-Gita, "even God." Rest is not about the couch and potato chip bag, it's about a way of being in the world of action. Small as grocery shopping, large as facing down the entrenched, faceless powers in our world that would do harm, the energy is the same. The whole relative world is in motion, always, and how we conduct ourselves within that current is how we find rest.

Notice in the logion that within the house, which stands for this center that we call our "selves", the man tests his strength, which is the energy of wisdom. He pierces his own walls—and we all have them. The walls between ourselves and others, ourselves and our environment, ourselves and what shadows we might hide within us are just few I can name easily. Like the flaming sword of the Tibetan Buddhist Bodhisattva Manjushri, the sword must first carve away our own ignorance before it can be used in any way "beyond us".

But the whole Gospel of Thomas has called that concept into question as well. Who are the "giants"? Nothing other than ourselves, in a different form, making different choices. Until we understand that the sword that pierces them pierces us as well, we will not be able to act with compassion, the other handle if you will, of a whole jug of spiritual maturity. If you look at most swords, the handle and hand-guards form a cross...we place our hand on this. The long blade shoves not just into flesh but the very ground of our being. Even God must act. But how do you act *as* God does, filled with wisdom and compassion, and find the effortlessness rest in every action? Do not leave your house to mete out justice, my friend, until you know the answer.

Ameyn.

The Eastern Parallels:

"One who thinks he kills or thinks he can be killed is dwelling in ignorance."

-- The Bhagavad-Gita

"All things must act, even God."

--The Bhagavad-Gita

Going Deeper:

What walls would you pierce within yourself with the sword of wisdom? What roles do wisdom and compassion play in seeing these parts of yourself? How does piercing those walls help you act in the world?

Summation:

We enter into rest when we first confront the walls within ourselves before we try to move decisively with wisdom and compassion in the world.

Logion 99

His students said to him,

**"Your brothers and
your mother are standing
just outside the door."**

**"My true mother and brothers
are those present right here
who fulfill my Father's desires.
It is they who will get into
my Father's realm," he replied.**

The First Response:

What voices wait outside your door,
outside this place,
where you have dusted
and arranged the cushions,
filled the larder with food
for your soul?
Some say, let all come in.
If you have built on a firm foundation,
if you know your walls
and ceilings and floors
deeply and well,
then you can throw open the windows,
hook the door wide,
and even the red and sticky mud on their feet
will not bother you
at all.

Today in Wisdom's Caravan:

Our house, our cave of the heart, becomes a place of rest when we are able to discern what voices within us serve a higher purpose and what voices do not, what voices are ours and what never were, what voices are companions and guests for the journey of our lives. We will find rest when we are able to wholly understand this.

We are easily swayed by the thoughts and actions of those closest to us, but they stand outside our house, our place of centering built on the foundation of wisdom and compassion. Until we can live out of this place, we have to learn our rest must come from closing the doors and windows to some. Most mystical traditions say this is a stage, though. At some point, we will be so firmly established that we will not need the wall and the sword because we will begin to live out of ultimate reality, out of that great Oneness of life.

Ameyn.

The Eastern Parallels:

"You may control a mad elephant;
You may shut the mouth of the bear and the tiger;
Ride the lion and play with the cobra;
By alchemy you may earn your livelihood;
You may wander through the universe incognito;
Make vassals of the gods; be ever youthful;
You may walk in water and live in fire;
But control of the mind is better and more difficult."

— Paramahansa Yogananda

Going Deeper:

What important friends do you let into the house of your self? What voices must you keep outside for the time being?

Summation:

We enter into rest when we begin to understand that we are the discerning gatekeepers to our own inner homes of mind and heart.

Logion 100

They showed him a gold coin and said,

"Caesar's agents
demand tribute
from us."

He said to them,
"Then give to Caesar
what is Caesar's.
Give to God
what is God's.
And give to me
that which is mine."

The First Response:

What if the inevitable for us all
is not death and taxes,
but rather
joy?
Why would we render anything unto Caesar
or
unto God
dividing the whole universe into
a pile of pulled threads
and slippery knots
that do not hold?
Here, sit at the loom,
and I can show you how to fold in a piece of ribbon,
no knots, no stitches keeping it in place,
just the passage of warp
and the way it is packed tightly with
the rest of the weft.
The cloth of Mystery does not bind,

separate
or
make such tiring distinctions--
it aligns and holds us all,
so we can wake up
and
truly rest.

Today in Wisdom's Caravan:

Would you rest? Then begin to see that Caesar and God and Yeshua are the self-created subdivisions of a greater unity. It takes tremendous effort to be for and against, to try to hold all the nuances of hierarchies and divisions and states of being. The one who rests is the one who sees through the effortful and painfully separating work of our analytic minds and finds that place of pure being.

This is not navel-gazing, nor burying your head in the sand. Yeshua is not saying, "don't pay your taxes." He's saying, "don't divide up your attention, wasting energy on the flux and flow of relative reality. See the Mystery in the money, in your "idea" of God, in the person before you, even as you act with the clear responsibility of the present moment. Look through both lenses and you will find the details of life effortless and filled with joy.

Ameyn.

The Eastern Parallels:

"As long as a human being worries about when he will die, and what he has that is his,
all of his works are zero.
When affection for the I-creature and what it owns is dead,
then the work of the Teacher is over."

— Kabir

"You have left Your Beloved and are thinking of others:
and this is why your work is in vain."

— Kabir

Going Deeper:

In what ways do you divide up your reality? Can you see how
much energy this takes? In what way could you use that energy
to be of benefit to yourself and others?

Summation:

**We enter into rest when we live out of the unity of our shared
existence, rather than quibble over the categories and
subtexts of life.**

Logion 101

Yeshua says,

"Whoever does not reject
father and mother
in the way I do
cannot be my student.
Whoever does not welcome
father and mother as I do
cannot be my disciple,
for my mother brought me forth,
but Truth gave me life."

The First Response:

The child must awaken.
The sleepy smiles and acquiescence
morph into the slammed door,
the silence.
It's not forever
and doesn't mean
he or she doesn't love you—
indeed,
without the walls
even the most well-meaning
parent consumes in the end
the delicate and separate
Becoming.

The butterfly-adult is only holding the tension
between the parent and their values
and
the deeper agape
that sees into the universal heart—

371

we love for the sake of God
in all things.

Today in Wisdom's Caravan:

Here we see the tensions being knit together—keeping
the societal values, the untruths we have picked up from our
kin, and the family dynamics that have wounded us at a distance
even as we love everyone deeply. This is a perfect example of
living in both relative and ultimate reality simultaneously, and
many therapists might see here the healthy individual psyche at
work.

All of us are flawed and what we absorb from each other
must be carefully filtered through a process of experience and
discernment. But at the same time, all of us are also perfect,
whole, the divine looking through us like an Icon. We are called
to hold both, and this holding is not effort-filled but restful. To
struggle against a person, to try to change them or ourselves is
wasted effort. This way of loving that Yeshua teaches meets the
person where he or she is, flawed and perfect at once and no
change is necessary beyond that deeper seeing.

Ameyn.

The Eastern Parallels:

"My God is love and sweetly suffers all."

— Sri Aurobindo

"The great are strongest when they stand alone,
A God-given might of being is their force."

— Sri Aurobindo

Going Deeper:

How do you work with the energy of loved ones who push their agendas or short-sighted views of the world upon you? What strategies do you use to both love and stay true to your own knowing and truth?

Summation:

We enter into rest when we are able to hold those we love with both a discerning distance and a recognition of our eternal oneness.

Logion 102

Yeshua says

"Cursed are your
religious leaders
for they are like dogs
sleeping in the feed bin.
They do not eat
nor do they allow
the cattle to eat."

The First Response:

He was a Christian,
he said,
until he actually read the Bible.
Years later,
I still puzzle at that;
not the push back,
no,
but the way he ran
hurt, bleeding, telling everyone,
unable to stand in the pain
of the imperfect human document,
all the while missing
the divine urge in humanity
that brought it forth.
He was probably nearer its heart than he realized
and nobody cuts us so deep
as our beloved images turned betrayer.

Today in Wisdom's Caravan:

This is a strongly worded logion, and a hint at the passion the human Yeshua feels when people are purposely treated as objects to be controlled. The priests of his day get a lot of heat in the Synoptic Gospels, too, and partially because he could see that even they did not learn from the knowledge they held so close to their chests. As we can see here, dogs cannot actually eat the cattle food they so jealously guard.

Cattle, in a herd, could easily oust the dogs, flipping them out of the bin with their horns and greater size, chasing the dogs away with their hard hooves and thick skins. But here, the herd is literally "cowed" and allowing it to happen. This is the dangerous side of behaviors that resemble rest—allowing abuse to happen and even calling it "godly" or "holy". Hence the strong language from Yeshua. We cannot love fully and well unless we first live out of the Kingdom and we cannot do that if do not first deeply consider the words of our religious leaders, texts, rituals, creeds, and dogmas. Having done that, if we decide to stay within an institution, we can then become a prophet and a force for good *within* the system. This is like loving our parents, but also standing up as an individual.

Ameyn.

The Eastern Parallels:

"Enlightenment is a destructive process. It has nothing to do with becoming better or being happier. Enlightenment is the crumbling away of untruth. It's seeing
through the facade of pretence. It's the complete eradication of everything we
imagined to be true."

— Adyashanti

"The Truth is the only thing you'll ever run into that has no agenda."

— Adyashanti

Going Deeper:

How do you hold the tension between your own way of seeing the divine, and the church community, ashram, temple, or synagogue you participate in? How do you respond to the anger aimed at religious leaders in this logion? What skills do you need to develop to stand in religious community and not be like the cattle kept from the feed bin?

Summation:

We enter into rest when we discern the difference between reigning in effortless awareness and the energy of passivity.

Logion 103

Yeshua says

"Blessed are those who are aware
of the approach of thieves,
who know when and where they will enter
even before they appear,
for then they can arise and prepare
by gathering their sovereignty
about them
binding to themselves
that which was there from the beginning."

The First Response:

She walks into the church
finds a seat in the midst of the chairs,
neither back nor front,
the middle of the scale
the note anyone can sing.

She arrives early,
closes her eyes,
even as the choir practices—
their imperfection is the best part,
the stops and starts
as the director hears something off
in that gathering of voices.

She can't hear anything wrong,
and that makes her smile
at the Mystery.

Today in Wisdom's Caravan:

This is the antidote to logion 102—the way to not be driven away from your feed bin in a sense. By living out of the sovereignty realized in the experiences of non-dual awareness, those who would try to steal from you—who try to take your creativity, your love, your individual expression of the Divine—are seen for what they are. Ironically this allows us to love the thieves in their own brokenness, even as we do not allow them to bend us to the ground with them. Like the way we love and yet see our parents for who they are, Yeshua is applying the same Aikido to the religious thieves of our world.

This is restful because there is no longer a struggle in the dark, no longer a flash of daggers cutting us nor is anything able to be taken from us. We see and can avoid that struggle even as we stay engaged with the relative world.

Ameyn.

The Eastern Parallels:

"Watch the too indignantly righteous. Before long you will find them committing or condoning the very offence which they have so fiercely censured."

— Sri Aurobindo

Going Deeper:

How do you find that place that is between hyper vigilance and calm and abiding awareness? What do you need to do for yourself to enter and maintain that sense of sovereignty?

Summation:

We enter into rest when we are able to see the world accurately from our sovereign seat of deep awareness, even as the actions of that world continue around and within us.

Logion 104

They said to Yeshua,

"Come, then,
Let us fast and pray."

He said to them,

"Have I sinned?
Have I been overcome?
No, only when the bridegroom
leaves the bridal chamber
will it be time to fast and pray."

The First Response:
There is an urge today,
to lay my head down on the keyboard.
Not to cry, no,
that would mean
a trip to the city to replace the tech—
it doesn't do well with salt and water
splashing on JKL;
rather,
the surgery drained something I'd taken for granted—
a nice, smooth round belly,
with fiery stretch marks, true,
and
my usually bounding energy that now
runs on three huge mugs of green tea.

It's all a passing piece of elevator music-
energy and the lack of it,
this new body and the way it looked a year ago,
and if I shut my eyes here,

filling my little sac of mostly water with
breath,
ruach,
and re-find
refine
the notes that hover always--
an internal sky alive with vibration,
melody that precedes words or songs or baby cries,
I will have my fast and prayer
and
will
enter into the bridal chamber where
the Beloved laughs and traces my scars
and helps me try on the different tattoos
of transformation.

Today in Wisdom's Caravan:

When we move out of our center, out of our sense of reigning with ease, that is the time to return to practices that re-ground us. Our sense of aloneness might be the trigger, as well as our agitation and sense of fearfulness or combativeness. Our Beloved has left the bridal chamber of our hearts (or so we think) and it's right and proper then to come back to prayer and abiding meditation and breath and fasts so that we re-awaken and return to Presence.

But such practices, done out of habit or with an eye toward being religiously correct do not bring rest; rather, they bring a sense of propriety, effort, willfulness. When abiding, simply abide. When you cannot, then return to the skills you have learned when you searched, found, worked with trouble and settled into wonder. This is the way of Yeshua's rest— skillful use of the *tools* of religion freed from the onus of obligatory practice.

Ameyn.

The Eastern Parallels:

". . . I feel we don't really need scriptures. The entire life is an open book, a scripture. Read it. Learn while digging a pit or chopping some wood or cooking some food. If you can't learn from your daily activities, how are you going to understand the scriptures? "

— Swami Satchidananda

"It's very simple. Keep your body as clean as possible, your mind as clear as possible. That's all you need. And do it in anyway you can, in your own way. It doesn't matter. That's why I say 'peaceful body, peaceful mind'. And then you'll be useful. You don't have to become a useful person. You will be useful."

— Swami Satchidananda

Going Deeper:

How do you know when the Bridegroom has left the bridal chamber, when you are out of balance and no longer abiding as a sovereign Presence in your world? What tools might you use to find your balance and center again?

Summation:

We enter into rest when we can use the tools of entering into presence at the right time and for the right reasons.

Logion 105

Yeshua says,

**"The one who knows
his true father and mother
will be called
the son of a whore."**

The First Response:

Language is a red cape,
flung before us,
the dust spattering into our eyes as we lunge,
our heavy horned heads sweeping
for the thin, fancy, irritating dancer
behind the veil.
It's not that we won't be hurt
if we can sweep it all aside--
we'll just be face to face with
the Real.

Today in Wisdom's Caravan:

While we might see the pain that reality has inflicted on Yeshua due to his "illegitimate" birth, we also should harken to the deeper spiritual notes here. When we birth the consciousness that allows us to see relative and ultimate reality in a glance, we do it without the physical intervention of another in our lives. We are all Mary, in a sense, and the child we birth is ourselves. In other words, we truly are born again from a virgin this time, the place of non-dual awareness.

Parts of the world may indeed react to such sovereignty and label you the child of a whore. The singleness, this label of

Ihidaya, (a term used to describe Yeshua which means "single one" or "unified one") is not controllable in the classic sociological sense and the emotions that can be created as the awakening person rubs up against the structures of their culture, time, and place can be incredibly painful.

It is restful when we realize that in this instance, the pain is a re-birthing, over and over, of our true Self. Like a mother in labor, we need not fear or loath the pain, but rather understand that soon we will cradle the child of our deepest Being.

Ameyn.

The Eastern Parallels:

"To preserve openness of heart and calmness of mind, nurture these attitudes:

Kindness to those who are happy
Compassion for those who are less fortunate
Honor for those who embody noble qualities
Equanimity to those whose actions oppose your values"

— Nischala Joy Devi

"We are missing much joy if we allow the world to dictate the direction of our thoughts and feelings. But when our heart guides the focus of our consciousness, love is ever present in our life."

-- Nischala Joy Devi

Going Deeper:

Have you experienced times of pain as you interact with others in society, pain that might be directly linked to the way you see and understand the world? How do you transmute that pain into joy and rest without disengaging from community?

Summation:

We enter into rest when we are able to see that the sometimes painful interactions in community are simply our continued birth-pains that are part of being a Unified One.

Logion 106

Yeshua says,

"When you are able
to transform
two into one,
then you, too, will become
"Son of Humanity,"
and it will be possible
for you to say to a mountain,
"Move," and it will move."

The First Response:

Superhumans move mountains
and really,
doesn't someone always end up dead then?
How we secretly long for such things—
strength to toss cars,
read someone's mind,
bend nature to our will,
but
keep scratching such an itch and
what you find
is
usually
a tight little ball of
isolation and fear.
The power to move mountains will not save you—
rather,
It is knowing *why* you want this
in the first place
that will be
your
rest.

Today in Wisdom's Caravan:

The child of the whore is the single one, transformed from two into one and who then becomes the child of all humanity, graced and empowered through his or her own re-birth. This is the "wisdom of the twin", the two who become aware that they are actually one, the dual nature of the world seen fully at last. Life becomes infinitely workable, mastery is not just subtle but also a profound mix of wisdom with compassion that births the ihidaya, the single one.

Knowing you can move mountains but also being aware of all the ramifications of your actions puts you in a place of rest. Great movements and small gestures are leveled, and the paradoxes resolved within you. Gold and bird seed husks become the same, shot through with Light. The mountain and you are one, so why move it? What is space, time, culture, and geography to one who is single and unified? They have all become Wa-hayye, life energy, the dance of God.

Ameyn.

The Eastern Parallels:

"The power of God is with you at all times, through the activities of mind, senses, breathing, and emotions, and is constantly doing all the work using you as a mere instrument."

--The Bhagavad-Gita

"The immature think that knowledge and action are different, but the wise see them as the same."

--The Bhagavad-Gita

Going Deeper:

What keeps you from moving the mountains of your life? Do you understand why you want them moved? What wisdom can you take away from all these words today, and what compassion?

Summation:

We enter into rest when, unified, we are wholly human and wholly divine, and the mountains are not any different from the ground on which we stand.

Logion 107

Yeshua says,

"The divine Realm
can be compared
to a shepherd
who had one hundred sheep.
One of the finest went astray,
so he left the ninety-nine
and went out searching
for it until he found it."
Troubled,
he said,
'I longed for you more than
the ninety-nine.'"

The First Response:

The one who breaks from the herd,
is
sometimes alone and fearful,
sometimes full of bravado,
sometimes simply
giggling with curiosity and wonder.
There is a difference between
what is right and
what is True,
and there will always be single sheep
who will get that,
who wander away,
small feet unerring on the hard stones.

In their solitary pilgrimage,
the Shepherd may spot them at last,

laughing,
"I have always loved
you
best."

Today in Wisdom's Caravan:

This particular parable of the lost sheep is not so much about God finding but rather God approving of the one who *can* separate from the herd and walk alone beyond instinctual action, beyond group-think and religious laws and the need to seek approval in numbers. When I teach yoga, I often have to revisit exercises that show how much we are influenced by the movements of people around us. The litany plays loudly in some of our minds—"is that particular student "better" than me? More poised? Better dressed? Do they get more attention? Should I move like that so I can be loved?" We seldom get a chance to feel what our practice is really like when we are caught up in being members of the herd.

The sheep who wanders off is at rest. She no longer needs the approval or support of the herd. This is not saying she is not lonely, and maybe a little fearful at times. It simply means she has to see herself without the mirror of others, move herself over the land at a pace that is her own, respond to her environment with discernment and decisive action. And yet, this single one finds she is also more deeply connected to her greatest safety net and undying support system, her union with God. The herd is a false safety, a false truth, a false knowing, and this little sheep gets that.

Ameyn.

The Eastern Parallels:

"The peace of God is with them whose mind and soul are in harmony, who are free from desire and wrath, who know their own soul."

--The Bhagavad-Gita

"The man who sees me in everything
and everything within me
will not be lost to me, nor
will I ever be lost to him."

--The Bhagavad-Gita

Going Deeper:

What herds do you belong to? What are the pros and cons of being in that community? What are the pros and cons of walking alone?

Summation:

We enter into rest when we, like a single sheep, can tread the paths of the world without a herd, unified with our Shepherd and our God.

Logion 108

Yeshua says,

"Whoever drinks
what flows
from my mouth
will come to be as I am
and I also will come
to be as they are,
so that what is hidden
may manifest."

The First Response:

Open my mouth,
a little bird beak,
catching dew,
the tongue anchored so
I might hear how those drops flow
down
outside coming in,
insides expanding,
the tissue between this and that
so very thin
a fledgling skin.
And if my eyes aren't quite ready to open
have mercy.
And if I can only take smalls sips at a time
have mercy
And if I am slow to open glorious wings like You
have mercy.
Lord you already know
you are my prayer.

Today in Wisdom's Caravan:

There is a sensual tenderness here, living water flowing from Yeshua to us on his words. The flow is not one way, for as we are changed, so is Yeshua. That is the deeper nature of relationship, the oiled pocket door joining two hallways that slides away to create a single passage. In that singleness, one cannot change without changing the other, because there is no "other." Alter the pattern, and it will echo through the whole design. Who is savior? Who is saved? It's always and forever a mutual becoming.

The rest is knowing that we are not really being changed, only awakening, maturing into what we already are. The rest becomes obvious when we realize we don't have to do it alone, because "alone" itself is the illusion. The rest flows over us when we stand united with God, who is also awakening, maturing, creating, the action in non-action, the rauch of breath, the ongoing creation.

Ameyn.

The Eastern Parallels:

"Curving back within myself I create again and again."

--The Bhagavad-Gita

"He who is rooted in oneness
realizes that I am
in every being; wherever
he goes, he remains in me.

When he sees all being as equal
in suffering or in joy
because they are like himself,
that man has grown perfect in yoga."

--The Bhagavad-Gita

Going Deeper:

What metaphors can you find in nature and science that support the idea that if you change one piece of the system the entire system itself changes? How does this relate to this logion? What does this say to you?

Summation:

We enter into rest when we abide in the Becoming that is action in non-action, knowing that there, all paradoxes cease in the deepest unity of relationship.

Logion 109

Yeshua says,

"The divine Realm
is like a man who owned
a field with treasure
hidden away in it.
Unaware of it, he died
leaving it to his son,
who also knew nothing about it.
After taking possession of the land,
the son practically gave
it away for nothing.
But the one who bought it
began plowing
and discovered the treasure,
and immediately started lending money at
interest to
whomever he pleased."

The First Response:

What treasure could you discover
that,
when you lend from your wealth
but at interest,
damages neither the lender or borrower?

A father had it but never knew,
his son passed it by,
and now you are called to go out in the field
breaking the ground by hand,
hoping only to sow and reap,

scattering grains in dry soil.

Lo, it is turned over by the blade,
shiny and new and
instantly you think
you can free the ox and hang the plough with flower baskets?
Pause here a moment
where actions can separate you
from the smell of this dark soil,
these seeds of wheat running between your fingers.

Just what is your treasure worth?

Today in Wisdom's Caravan:

Throughout the Gospel of Thomas, and the Synoptics as
well, there is an injunction to not lend at interest, to be healed
and not to tell, to share gnosis freely for those wanting and able
to receive it. The language of this logion, then, is curious
indeed. To me it is a warning—that the treasure we find, this
place of Union, can be put back into the ego-work of increasing,
using the other, and leaving the Father's ever-rich field. Our
rest then becomes coldly vocational, separating, and alienating.
Rest is when the treasure is the secret of the field,
nestled within it like a yolk in an egg shell. It will not make us
wealthy, cannot be used to artificially separate one from
another nor herd us all together under a rubric of law and
custom and dogma. Look deeply into the field you might give
away—perhaps the religion itself that you feel is unredeemable,
the words that have become arid, the friendships that seem dry.
The treasure is there, perfect in its hidden nature and beyond
the exhausting ways of commerce and power.
Ameyn.

The Eastern Parallels:

"*We* read the world wrong and say that it deceives us."

— Rabindranath Tagore

Going Deeper:

How do you react when you have a new insight, or are aware of a new level of being within yourself? What are the consequences of those reactions?

Summation:

We enter into rest when we are content to abide with the treasure of gnosis without lending it at interest to the dividing powers of commerce and status.

Logion 110

Yeshua says,

"Whoever finds the cosmos
and becomes rich
must ultimately let the cosmos go."

The First Response:

At eighteen,
I never would have guessed
that my riding and art and showmanship trophies
might end up in the dumpster,
the ribbons that once ran the circuit of my room,
squashed together and thrown out
with mash potatoes and steak bones,
my old Miss Thunder Bay sash
wadded up in some corner of my
son's dresser to plug a hole.
It wasn't a painful letting go—
just so much plastic and faux-marble,
just so much fake silk and yellow thread—
and I need less tangible things now
to mirror the worth of my existence.

Today in Wisdom's Caravan:

Now the intent of Logion 109 becomes much more clear.
If the richness of ourselves, our gnosis, is turned to profiting in
the ways of the world, that requires us to eventually release
such things if we are to rest. The treasure Yeshua is hoping we
discover within us is so much more than working with the
energies of relative reality in a way that is profit-oriented. The
richness resides in our being, not in any particular change as
such.

The fallow field is not fallow at all. But *is* the treasure pulled out into the ways of commerce and superficial relationship and power a treasure *worth* having any longer? It has becomes a blight, a weight, and a hindrance, bound by the dictates of time, place, and culture. In a sense, if we see this, we begin cradle what is hidden, nurture what will not be applauded, rest with what will never bring us wealth in the traditional sense.

And that is the best treasure of all, the breastplate that cannot be taken from you ever.

Ameyn.

The Eastern Parallels:

"When one's mind dwells on the objects of senses, fondness for them grows on him, from fondness comes desire, from desire, anger. Anger leads to bewilderment, bewilderment to loss of memory of true Self, and by that, intelligence is destroyed, and with the destruction of intelligence, he perishes."

--The Bhagavad-Gita

"To him [the Sage], what seemeth the bright things of day to the mass, are known to be the things of darkness and ignorance—and what seemeth dark as night to the many, he seeth suffused with the light of noonday."

--The Bhagavad-Gita

Going Deeper:

How does it feel to go through the stages of searching, finding, trouble, wonder and reigning, but never profit from it in the way of the world? Be honest with the words or images that come.

Summation:

We enter into rest when we understand our kingdom and treasure, our gnosis in other words, is worth more to us than the value assigned such things in relative reality.

Logion 111

Yeshua says,

"Heaven and earth
will completely disappear
in your presence,
and the one who lives by means
of the Living One
will not see death,
because, as Yeshua says,
"The cosmos is not worthy of the one
who discovers the Self."

The First Response:

Oh, my friend,
it's never this or that,
and saying the right thing
must include the wrong by design.
Musical notes hang on their lines
but the melody evoked, where does it rest?
The brush strokes are but sea-foam to the ocean
of the artist's vision,
and when I tuck my child in,
even though he's 14 and resistant to such things,
it is the silence of the dark that he nestles into
because a fragile presence has made it
loving and safe.

Today in Wisdom's Caravan:

This logion is about as close as you can come to
articulating non-dual consciousness using largely Christian
language. Heaven and earth are brought together in a single

point, and living out of that singleness, death is also transcended with the rest of the paradoxes of our journey. The fear that motivates our greed, our violence, our neediness is all incorporated within this larger Self, the True Self, as Thomas Merton called it.

The rest comes as a direct energy of this transformation; all the things we struggle with are unified and made whole within us. Nothing is neglected or rejected, nothing held up as a trophy or award. This leveling is not about losing anything that makes us juicy human beings though! It simply means that the shadows of our lives are now soaked in light and we have become steady, conscious and awake. Ameyn.

The Eastern Parallels:

"We realize--often quite suddenly--that our sense of self, which has been formed and constructed out of our ideas, beliefs and images, is not really who we are. It doesn't define us, it has no center."

— Adyashanti,

"The way they perceive the world suddenly changes, and they find themselves without any sense of separation between themselves and the rest of the world."

— Adyashanti

Going Deeper:

How do you react when you think of heaven and earth and death all passing away? What does this mean in your own words?

Summation:

We enter into rest when all the parts of ourselves come together in wholeness, allowing heaven and earth and death to all pass away.

Logion 112

Yeshua says,

*"Wretched is the flesh
that is dependent upon the soul,
and the soul that is
dependent upon the flesh."*

The First Response:

If our hand never stroked
the imperfect skin of our lover,
looked into gray eyes
and watched, later
the sod fall on the coffin,
a lifetime flashed and glimmered and gone,
what use the soul then?

If we had never paused,
picnic spread out in the graveyard,
and wondered, wandered
out beyond such things
as beginnings and endings
this and that,
never learned to pray and BE,
what use this body then?

Do not be so quick to stop living a full life;
do not be so satisfied to ignore the
urge to search
and find
and be troubled
and to wonder
and reign

so one day, you will rest
in dynamic fullness
indeed.

Today in Wisdom's Caravan:

Yeshua is trying very hard to show in this Logion the power that he himself represents, the fully embodied human who is also fully in union with God. Humankind errs on either side, falling into pure body consciousness or trying to ignore the body wholly in favor of the "spirit". Neither works quite simply because neither is reality-as-such. We are embodied. We are Spirit. And until those two pieces slide together seamlessly, there will always be struggle, confusion, anger and loneliness. Truly, Yeshua is giving us the very recipe for rest.

The impulse to move either way, more toward the body or more toward the spirit should alert us to a wound we are carrying within us, an inability to be vulnerable to some part of ourselves. Yeshua is as much healer as wisdom teacher, or prophet or "savior". We are given such a great opportunity here to re-find and refine the natural balance of body and spirit that God intended for us.

Ameyn.

The Eastern Parallels:

"All that is real in me is God; all that is real in God is I. The gulf between God and human beings is thus bridged. Thus we find how, by knowing God, we find the kingdom of heaven within us."

--Swami Vivekananda

"As long as we believe ourselves to be even the least different from God, fear remains with us; but when we know ourselves to be the One, fear goes; of what can we be afraid? As soon as

I think that I am a little body, I want to preserve it, to protect it, to keep it nice, at the expense of other bodies; then you and I become separate."

--Swami Vivekanda

Going Deeper:

Do you feel you err one way or the other, more toward spirit or more toward body? Why do you think this might be so? Is there a wound you can point to that makes this more understandable to you?

Summation:

We enter into rest when we function out of the place that is equally of spirit and embodied being.

Logion 113

His students asked him,

"On what day
will the kingdom
arrive?"

"Its coming cannot be perceived
from the outside," he said.
"You cannot say,
'Look, it's over there' or
'No, here it is.'
The father's realm
is spreading out
across the face of the earth
and humanity is not able
to perceive it."

The First Response:

Do you sometimes wonder
why he did not weep more in his aloneness?
The disciples he had called,
falling asleep outside in the Garden,
mumbling to themselves
dreams of power,
poised just over that ridge,
just behind this drooping eyelid.
Alone he went to his trial
and to his cross
and to his tomb,
or rather
surrounded by one-eyed men and women
who never really learned

to brush the crusted sands of
sleep
away.

Today in Wisdom's Caravan:

I often hear the human Yeshua sprinkled through these sayings, sometimes laughing and sometimes at the very edge of his patience. Here, he is bluntly telling them what he has been trying to show through parable and his living presence—heaven is right here, earth is right here, together, they are one and this is what it means to be whole. There are times I feel so deeply for him—the loneliness he must have experienced as he tried again and again to bring people into the brilliant, fearless, fully alive world he knew intimately. I think he largely failed to convey the vastness of his vision, and he knew that, too.

The lesson of rest here is knowing at what point to be blunt; to give away the whole enchilada and then let go. As we shall see in the next logion, the key to *that* is to come back to a sense of humor and spaciousness rooted in human relationships and contact.

Ameyn.

The Eastern Parallels:

"Today it is heaped at your feet, it has found its end in you
The love of all man's days both past and forever:
Universal joy, universal sorrow, universal life.
The memories of all loves merging with this one love of ours -
And the songs of every poet past and forever."

--Rabindranath Tagore

Going Deeper:

How do you react when you are misunderstood? What tools do you use to communicate with others? What new tools would you like to learn?

Summation:

We enter into rest when, after sharing our view of the world to those who ask, simply let any expectation of understanding go.

Logion 114

Simon Peter said to them all,

"Mary should leave us
for women are not
worthy of this Life."

Yeshua said,

"Then I myself will lead her,
making her male
if she must becomes
worthy of you males!
I will transform her
into a living spirit
because any woman changed
in this way
will enter the divine Realm."

The First Response:

That he should end this journey joking,
poking fun, and laughing quietly to himself.
That he should settle down,
Mary's hand in his own
squeezing it to let her know
for a time
he was there,
that he knew she knew
that *they* still didn't know,
and even then have the sense
to tell them one more time,
the divine realm will heat us and mix us
wild atoms thrown into form

the energy of our love
speaking down through the corn fields
and in the eyes of lovers
long after the sun
expands and devours us whole,
the music will flow on
unimpeded and waiting
only
for ears
that
hear.

Today in Wisdom's Caravan:

If the previous logion was laced with impatience, this one actually shows an even clearer glimmer of what it might have been like to learn at the knee of Yeshua—humor, gentle chiding, including everyone effortlessly into relationship, even when the situation is so hot that feminists today still rage at this saying. He is teaching us how to laugh, the highest and best litmus test for intelligence and understanding, as well as showing us the best way to rest. Be spacious, inclusive, discerning, gentle and fearless in your relationships because then you become the living "proof" of everything Yeshua is trying to teach.

It is fascinating that we end with this logion, this snapshot of how to be in the world *and* "be" spiritual. Some authors also see that this as a call to go forward and read the *Gospel According to Mary Magdalene,* a text that would have been in circulation about the same time as this Gospel of Thomas. However you see it, I hope you are smiling away with me, here at the end of our journey together.

Now, the work is in your hands. If you are called, I hope you do as I have done, take a logion a day and walk for a while beside Yeshua. Scripture of any kind is only as alive as its readers, only as dynamic as what is put into practice by the living, only as holy as it is able to lead us to a tangible wholeness.

Ameyn.

The Eastern Parallels:

"I am looking at you
You at him,
Kabir asks, how to solve
this puzzle—
You, he and I?"

"I am not a Hindu,
Nor a Muslim am I!
I am this body, a play
of five elements, a drama
of the spirit dancing
with joy and sorrow."

--Kabir

Going Deeper:

How do you make use of humor and honesty together in your interactions in the world? What "tips" can you see in this logion to help you in your daily relationships?

Summation:

We enter into rest when we are spacious, inclusive, discerning, gentle, humor-filled and fearless in our relationships, becoming the living proof of all that Yeshua has tried to teach.

We enter into Rest when...

96. we yeast our lives with simplicity, an honest relationship with everything and a sense of transparency.

97. we move in the world of actions with both wisdom and compassion.

98. we first confront the walls within ourselves before we try to move decisively with wisdom and compassion in the world.

99. we begin to understand that we are the discerning gatekeepers to our own inner homes of mind and heart.

100. we live out of the unity of our shared existence rather than quibble over the categories and subtexts of life.

101. we are able to hold those we love with both a discerning distance and a recognition of our eternal oneness.

102. we discern the difference between reigning in effortless awareness and the dulling energy of passivity.

103. we are able to see the world accurately from our sovereign seat of deep awareness, even as the actions of that world continue around us.

104. we can use the tools of entering into presence at the right time and for the right reasons.

105. we are able to see that our sometimes painful interactions in community are simply the continued birth-pains that are part of being a Unified One.

106. unified, we are wholly human and wholly divine, and the mountains are not any different from the ground on which we stand.

107. we, like a single sheep, can tread the paths of the world without a herd, unified with our Shepherd and our God.

108. when we abide in the Becoming that is action in non-action, knowing that there, all paradoxes cease, in the deepest unity of relationship.

109. we are content to rest with the treasure of gnosis without lending it at interest to the dividing powers of commerce and status.

110. we understand our kingdom and treasure, our gnosis, is worth more to us than the value assigned such things in relative reality.

111. all the parts of ourselves come together in wholeness, allowing heaven and earth and death to all pass away

112. when we function out of the place that is equally of spirit and embodied being.

113. after sharing our view of the world with those who ask, simply let any expectation of understanding go.

114. we are spacious, inclusive, discerning, gentle, humor-filled and fearless in our relationships, becoming the living proof of all that Yeshua has tried to teach.

Ameyn.

Sources

Adyashanti: (1962-) A modern teacher of both meditation and non-dual consciousness, this dynamic writer and speaker began his journey in the Zen tradition, but downplays any standard affiliations. He pulls regularly from all the world religious traditions, from Christianity to Vedanta to Buddhism, inviting his students into the raw experience of non-dual reality. His most recent books include *Resurrecting Jesus* and *Falling into Grace.*

Albert Einstein: (March 14, 1879-April 18 1955) This German-born theoretical physicist published over 300 scientific papers and 150 non-scientific writings. He can be counted as part of the new wave of scientists whose forays into physics lad to a deepened appreciation for the metaphoric nature of scripture— that science and religion share the concept of a search, although with different languages. Never a believer in a personal God, his agnostic writings are profoundly aimed at the call to care for our neighbor AS ourselves.

Sri Aurobindo: (August 15, 1872- December 5, 1950). This poet, philosopher, nationalist and yogi is best known for his vast vision of the purpose of man, which is not simply to become united with God, but also, to serve as a beacon of sanity and change in the world. His Sri Aurobindo Ashram is still in existence and his huge corpus of work continues to influence Integral thinkers the world over.

Bhagavad-Gita: This work, sometimes called in the west the Hindu Bible, is a tiny part of the much larger epic called *The Mahabharata*. In it, Krishna, the embodied avatar of God, teaches various yogas (ways of union with God) to Arjuna, a skilled archer of "one-pointed focus". It is notable especially for its message that all may participate in the dance with God, not simply the ordained or caste-bound religious professionals of our societies and that there are many paths to God.

Brihadaranyaka Upanishad: Its name means the Great Wilderness Upanishad and it is the stage for the great sayings and wisdom of the sage Yajnavalkya. It is also known as the source for non-dual chants and mantras about Brahman (the Godhead), including both Om Purna Mayam and Asato ma sat gamaya lines that are still sung and taken deeply to heart today. Most scholars date this work later than 6th Century BCE.

Chandogya Upanishad: One of the oldest of the Upanishads and held in highest regard through Indian history, this work dates from well before the 6th century BCE. It is ripe with high philosophy ranging from the meaning of OM to the important *mahavalkya*: Tat Tvam Asi or "Thou Art That".

The Dhammapāda: Thought to originate with the 3rd century BCE communities of India's Buddhist monks, this work is one of the most read and loved scriptures, with many translations in English. This simple collection of sayings is much like the Gospel of Thomas, without a great deal of narrative discourse clouding the sayings of the Buddha.

Dilgo Khyentse Rinpoche: (1910-September 28, 1991) Tibetan Buddhist scholar, teacher, poet and once head of the Tibetan Nyingma sect. He was one of the great jewels that came out of the Tibetan Diaspora, helping to preserve and spread the teachings of the Vajrayana Buddhist Path. This teacher left a number of Western-accessible books about Tibetan Buddhist life and practice, including *Enlightened Courage: An explanation of Atisha's Seven-Point Mind Training.*

Zen Master Dogen: (January 9, 1200-September 22, 1253). Japanese monk who founded the Soto School of Zen Buddhism. He's known for his work the *Shobogenzo* which contains 95 short lessons about Zen practice.

Eknath Easwaran: (December 17, 1910-October 26, 1999) Translator of Indian texts, meditation teacher and prolific writer, he established the Blue Mountain Center of Meditation. His mantra technique is called Passage Meditation, and is open and affirming of all other faith traditions and scripture.

The Flower Sermon: Known as the *Nemgenisho* (*pick up flower, subtle smile sutra*), this Zen classic illustrates the mind-to-mind transmission of awakening that does not depend upon words and abstract concepts to express truth. It may have originated with Chinese Chan Buddhists in the 14th century CE.

Swami Iraianban: Author of *Preaching Vedanta* is a lecturer and writer associated with IRAI (the Institute of Self-Realization), Tamil Nadu, India.

Heart Sutra: Created sometime between the 6th and 8th Century in China, this Buddhist text is part of the philosophical tradition of Mahayana Buddhism, and is particularly important to both Chan and Zen schools. It shows the interpenetration of relative and ultimate reality.

Isa (Isha) Upanishad: One of the smallest of the Upanishads, it dates from between 500-100 BCE. It uses the word Lord at the beginning, which many scholars associate with the later Bhakti (devotional yoga) movements in India. However, its content tends to be very much a monistic treatment of the divine.

Kabir: (1440-1518). This simple weaver was a skilled poet and songwriter who deeply influenced the bhakti movement (the path of devotion to God) in Northern India. He walked the line between Hinduism and Islam, and people from both traditions honored him, even as he, with great wit and deep feeling, denied that God was associated with any one religion. Nearly 9.6 million people continue to follow the Path of Kabir (Kabir Panth) today.

Katha Upanishad: Sometimes translated as "Death as the Teacher", this classic narrative Upanishad has been commented on for generations. It is associated with the Yajur Veda, and is thought to have been composed around the 5th century BCE.

Kena Upanishad: (6th Century BCE). This member of the 108 principle Upanishads is composed in both poem and narrative prose form, and is best known for its assertion that God is the energy that allows sight, hearing and all the rest. This is different from the eyeball or ear itself or the mind that makes "meaning". That one power is in us all and is indivisible.

Lynn Bauman: Scholar, writer, and contemplative, this man has worn many hats and has lived in both the United States and the Middle East. His translation of the Gospel of Thomas and his discovery of the metaframe that gives the work its coherence have been instrumental to helping people successfully approach this difficult text.

The Mahabharata: Scholars place the origin of the Mahabharata between the 6th and 8th Centuries BCE, although it may not have reached its final form until the 4th century CE. This enormous epic is seven times the size of the Iliad and Odyssey combined, and is the source of the Bhagavad-Gita. It follows the righting of dharma (Truth, Law) in a land out of balance. It is said that if you cannot find something in the Mahabharata, it simply does not exist.

Mirabai: (1498-???) Passionate woman poet and saint, who left nearly 1300 love poems to Krishna and who danced ecstatically in public at time when women did not do such things. Her work is translated the world over.

Mundaka Upanishad: Associated with the Artharva Veda, this work is given in a mantram form, but it is not used as a ritual text but rather a deep exploration of the knowledge of Brahman

(God). One of the principle 108 Upanishads, it is quite old (6th Century BCE or later) and focuses a great deal on the principle of the atman (the God-seed, if you will, within us all).

Neil Douglas-Klotz: Language scholar and Sufi, this prolific writer, musician and teacher has done much to help the Christian West rethink the meaning behind the Aramaic words of Yeshua. His best-known work is *Prayers of the Cosmos*.

Nischala Joy Devi: Dynamic modern teacher of therapeutic yoga, meditation and the path of devotion, this skilled teacher has done much to empower women over the course of her career. Her books include *The Secret Path of Yoga* and *The Healing Path of Yoga*.

The Parable of the Burning House: This narrative appears in Chapter 3 (the Hiyu Chapter) of the *Lotus Sutra*, and dates between 100 BCE and 200 CE. The Lotus Sutra is the most popular scripture of Mahayana Buddhism, used particularly with the Tien-tai and Nichiren schools (Pure Land Buddhism sects).

Sant Ravidas: (1450-1520 CE) This cobbler by trade became one of the best-loved mystics and poets of North India. He claimed that everyone has a right to worship God and read holy texts, not just those of certain castes, and that one's actions in the world make the person.

Sri Ramakrishna: (Feb 18, 1936-August 16, 1886) This unschooled and ecstatic Indian mystic was remarkable for his time—he practiced both Christianity and Islam as well as his native Hinduism and pronounced that all such paths led to the same realization of God. His work spun off many ashrams that aimed their work at bettering the lives of the people of India.

Sri Ramana Maharshi: (December 30, 1879-April 14, 1950) This Self-Awakened master yogi and teacher from Tamil Nadu is widely regarded as one of the finest sages of this age. He approved many paths to union, but especially spoke about self-inquiry—"who am I?"—as a way to peel away the layers of our egos and touch the continuous presence of the divine within. He did not create any images nor was devoted to any particular form of God.

Sri Sharada Devi: (1853-1920) The wife of Ramakrishna, considered an enlightened being in her own right. She outlived her husband by 34 years and was instrumental in helping the young Ramakrishna Order keep its course and flourish.

Sue Sutherland-Hanson, M.Div.: serves the Pacific Northwest, focusing on exploring and expressing the gift of our lives through creativity and using that lens to develop an authentic relationship with the Christian Tradition. She presides over rites of passage such as weddings and funerals, and is deeply committed to her contemplative path. Google her for more information about her classes and ministry.

Swami Satchidananda: (December 22, 1914-August 19, 2002). This dynamic man was the founder of the Integral Yoga Institute and Yogaville (both which continue to flourish today) in the United States. Swami was a delightful author who was able to translate the yogas and philosophies of India with a decidedly Western flavor and eye toward application. His books include deep looks at Patanajali's *Yoga Sutras* and the *Bhagavad-Gita*.

Shankara: (788 CE-820 CE): One of the best known teachers of India, this young man traveled from coast to coast, working with the system of Advaita (Non-Dual) Vedanta and entering into spirited discourse with both Buddhist and the proponents of other Hindu paths. His writings were quite vast, including commentaries on the Upanishads and Bhagavad-Gita.

Shvetashvatara Upanishad: (3rd or 4th Century BCE). The first of the Upanishads to elevate Shiva to the position of the supreme Lord (Ishvara) of the cosmos and may well be the birth-text of the Shaivite devotional movement in India that continues to this day.

Sivananda Saraswati: (September 8, 1887-July 14, 1963). This esteemed teacher of yoga and Vedanta founded schools and ashrams, the most notable being the Divine Life Society, and wrote over 200 books on Yoga and other topics. He has deeply influenced the philosophy and practice of Hatha Yoga in the United States.

Swami Swahananda: (June 29, 1921-October 19, 2012). The once-spiritual head of the Vedanta Society of Southern California wrote many works to further the spirit and intent of Advaita Vedanta philosophy and included topics that touched on the Mother, Swami Vivekananda, and other important figures of the path and institutions founded on the teachings of Shri Ramakrishna.

Rabindranath Tagore: (May 7, 1861-August 7, 1941) This Nobel Laureate in Literature (1913) is best known for his work *Gitanjali.* He founded the Visva Bharati University which continues to this day. He created many new poem and song forms and meters, dramas, and novels using his native language in ways that were fresh and ringing with deep devotional qualities. Much of his work focused on the independence of India, and contains universalist and humanist themes as well.

The Ramayana: Thought to date from the 4th or 5th century BCE, this fast-paced and enchanting work is one of two great epic works of India, the other being the Mahabharata. It lays out the ideals of the Indian culture—husband and wife, ruler and warrior, and relationship with the divine, but all framed against a fantastic background of monkey soldiers and wife-stealing demons. It is still held in high regard to this day.

Taittiriya Upanishad: (5th or 6th century BCE). This work is broken into sections about morality, the sheaths of embodied being, and ends with a narrative sequence in which a son, instructed by his father, grows deeper and more skillfully into his inquiry of the nature of Brahman (God).

Thich Nhat Hanh: (October 11, 1926-) This Vietnamese Buddhist monk, peace activist, poet, teacher and writer was friends with such US luminaries as Martin Luther King Jr. and Thomas Merton. His primary work centers on non-violent activism, and he is particularly skilled in the psychological healing of soldiers both East and West. His many books are accessible and insightful, filled with concrete practices and poetic inspiration.

Rev. Dr. Thomas Thresher: Serves as the pastor for the Suquamish United Church of Christ and has been involved in Integral Studies for many years. His book *Reverent Irreverence* is an important study about applying Ken Wilber's Integral Theory to actual churches. Tom is also actively involved in reframing religion as a vehicle for the evolution of consciousness, as well as writing and teaching about sustainable economic models.

Swami Vivekananda: (Jan 12, 1863-July 4, 1902) This best-known disciple of Shri Ramakrishna was one of the first to bring the teachings of Advaita Vedanta to the West, and in a form accessible to our broader culture. As a speaker, he filled huge lecture halls all over the country, and many of the Vedanta Societies he help found are vital and active even today.

Paramamsa Yogananda: (January 5, 1893- March 7, 1952). One of the most influential of the Eastern teachers in America and Europe, this man is best known for his introduction of the path of Kriya Yoga to the West. His work, *The Autobiography of a Yogi* has been translated into 34 languages and made the list of the top 100 most influential spiritual books of the century.

Yogavasishtha: (13 or 14th Century CE, but roots of a much older source text exist) Slightly smaller than the Mahabharata and said to take place chronologically prior to the Ramayana, this work tells the story of the teachings given from Valmiki to Rama, who was suffering from a kind of spiritual depression.

About the Author

Kimberly Beyer-Nelson holds a master's degree in comparative religion and a certificate in holistic healthcare from Western Michigan University. For over twenty years she has taught Hatha Yoga, Qigong and meditation. An internationally published poet, essayist, novelist and artist, she lives with her son and husband on Bainbridge Island in the Pacific Northwest.

You can visit her blog at
http://guhacaveoftheheart.blogspot.com/

Made in the USA
Monee, IL
19 April 2022

94995691R00246